BOOKS BY FRITZ PETERS

AVAILABLE THROUGH
VANITAS VANITATUM PUBLISHING

NOVELS
The World Next Door
Finistère
The Descent

~~~~~~

MEMOIRS
Boyhood with Gurdjieff
Gurdjieff Remembered

GURDJIEFF

REMEMBERED

BY FRITZ PETERS

VANITAS VANITATUM
PUBLISHING
LOS ANGELES

VANITAS VANITATUM PUBLISHING
LOS ANGELES, CALIFORNIA
6300 Canoga Avenue, Suite 1330 | Woodland Hills, CA 91367
www.vanitasvanitatum.com

The Fritz Peters Collection
Managing Editor: Alexandra Carbone
Cover Design: Mathieu Carratier
Typesetting: Stewart A. Williams

First Published: London: Victor Gollancz, 1965

ISBN 978-1-957241-10-4 / 1-957241-11-1
ISBN COLLECTION 978-1-957241-00-5

LCCN 2023916484

INTRODUCTION

Introduction

By Roger Lipsey

IT IS IMPOSSIBLE TO EXAGGERATE the impact of these two books when they were published in 1964 – 65, and their lasting impact to this day. They are treasures of the Gurdjieff literature. Though I'm sure there are differences of opinion, I consider them Fritz Peters' masterworks, a permanent gift to later generations. The first book, *Boyhood with Gurdjieff*, concerns Fritz's education in early adolescent years, ages 11 through 15, when Gurdjieff was his mentor and surrogate father, the compelling center of his life. The setting for their extraordinary relationship was Gurdjieff's Institute for the Harmonious Development of Man, founded by him in late 1922 at a quite beautiful manor house in Fontainebleau-Avon, a forested region outside of Paris. The second book, *Gurdjieff Remembered*, narrates his renewed encounters with Gurdjieff starting in the early 1930s and continuing into the 1940s, when he returned from the war nearly in a state of nervous breakdown and sought Gurdjieff's help.

Both books are powerful acts of memory. Fritz's recollections of incidents, words spoken, and his own responses are vividly authentic and detailed, not by a skilled writer's invention—though that he possessed—but by something else. Those who know from other sources Gurdjieff's way of life and eloquent but grammatically precarious English recognize that Gurdjieff is authentically here, though Fritz was writing decades later. Fritz himself offers the best explanation: speaking of Gurdjieff's lectures and informal talks in those early years, he reports that "not only did we not forget what he said to us, it was usually impossible to forget what he had said, even if one wished to forget it." Something like this extended to the whole of life around Gurdjieff: unforgettable, unforgotten.

Young Fritz, age 11, was nearly an orphan—he could easily feel this was so—but surrounded by a constellation of well-meaning adults, all of whom belonged to a circle of avant-garde writers and artists of the 1920s whose names are part of history. Margaret Anderson and Jane Heap, coeditors of the leading-edge American literary journal *The Little Review*, adopted Fritz when his estranged birth parents proved unable to care for him, though they would episodically do their best. Another surrogate parent was Gertrude Stein, author, matriarch of a unique literary-artistic salon, far-sighted art collector, friend and patron to Picasso and Hemingway, stable center in a whirling world. She decided with characteristic firmness that Fritz's education should include days in Paris with her—what a guide to the sights and meanings of the city! Thanks to her and her partner Alice B. Toklas, Fritz would spend time in passing with people he surely took for granted—I'm thinking of the sculptor Constantin Brancusi—that any of us would have given a great deal to know. Fritz was the smallest, but an intensely alive and inquiring object in a world that shaped key features even of today's culture, let alone the Modernist culture of the 1920s.

Jane and Margaret's decision to board their charge, Fritz, at the Gurdjieff institute was an avant-garde decision. The institute was a radically novel school for adults, dedicated to teaching a new, intensely practical approach to personal development, a new vision of human possibility that could be embodied and lived. There were, however, kids, the children of resident students, of Gurdjieff's brother and extended family, and of Gurdjieff himself—enough to make a mostly cheerful band who helped with the day-to-day maintenance of the school, its kitchen, gardens, and animals, and received in return an education one can only envy. Though Fritz's brother Tom remains in these books a somewhat shadowy figure—who knows what sibling rivalry prevailed—Tom was alongside Fritz through much of the adventure to come.

Readers coming to these two books in the new edition of Peters' writings may be unfamiliar with Gurdjieff and the institute. Both topics are nearly inexhaustible; here, thank goodness, we can look at them for the most part through Fritz's good eyes, but some context will be helpful. George Ivanovich Gurdjieff (1866 – 1949) was born in Alexandropol (now Gyumri, Armenia) and raised in what is now the Turkish city of Kars, where the Russian archpriest and dean of the local military church and school recognized his promise and took his education in hand. He was educated in Russian, while as a matter of course he was fluent in the Greek spoken in his family, in Armenian and Turkish, and later to some degree in Georgian and Farsi—languages reflecting the cultural richness of the region where he was born and raised. His father was an *ashokh*, a traditional bard with what must have been a vast repertory of tales and recitations, typically accompanied by a stringed instrument. Gurdjieff's autobiographical work, *Meetings with Remarkable Men*, picks up the story from that early point. Witness to mysteries he could not explain in the life around him and impelled by an innate need to understand what he spoke of as "the sense and aim of existence," Gurdjieff set off as a young man with a band of multi-talented Seekers of Truth—their chosen name—to discover whatever hidden, fundamental knowledge remained extant in the monasteries, brotherhoods, and indigenous cultures especially of Central Asia. It was a well-timed venture: Russian and British colonialism were encroaching on ancient lands and cultures, destructive wars lay ahead, and the homogenizing influence of the West on distinctive cultures would soon be felt, but much was still intact. There was a kind of privacy of cultures.

Gurdjieff and his companions journeyed for some twenty years. Gurdjieff learned in depth from encounters across Asia as far as

Tibet and India, as well as in Egypt and Ethiopia and in Orthodox Christian monasteries of Greece and the Near East. He also witnessed sacred dances and heard their music—this would prove to be important later, at the institute, where he choreographed a remarkable repertory of sacred dances and gymnastics for his students and composed music collaboratively with Thomas de Hartmann, a young, already celebrated composer. While this was a journey toward knowledge surviving among peoples and spiritual communities, it was also the long occasion for the development and maturation of Gurdjieff's independent understanding. When he took up residence in 1912 in what was for him the cultural-political center, Moscow and St. Petersburg, he offered a new teaching, not merely a synthesis from his travels though of course related to all he had learned as a pilgrim among cultures and teachers of many faiths and Ways. The man had genius; what he had encountered became fuel for a new vision and practice learned in part in the East but addressed to the West and responsive to Western tradition reaching back as far as the cosmology and rigorous lifestyle of the legendary Pythagoras. "Take the understanding of the East and the knowledge of the West—and then seek." This was an aphorism formulated by Gurdjieff some years later at the institute near Paris, and this he had accomplished. Today's students of his teaching continue to hear these words.

The teaching wasn't only words and ideas, though there were many new ideas brilliantly captured by Gurdjieff's Russian pupil, the author P. D. Ouspensky, whose record of Gurdjieff's talks in the Russian years was published in English just at the end of Gurdjieff's life as *In Search of the Miraculous*. The teaching was also—and you might say, centrally—about something little considered in the West at the time, still marginal today. Call it being, presence, self-awareness: a relaxed consolidation of the energies of mind, feeling, and body, a state of awakening that must be earned. Gurdjieff himself was changed by his discoveries and the work on himself he had willingly undergone. He had become a master. This is a term rarely used in English, likely off-putting except when we speak of the master of an artisanal craft or of a skill such as virtuoso musicianship, or of the master of an oceangoing vessel. It's the best term, all the same. Fritz instinctively recognized and learned from Gurdjieff's mastery of an encompassing craft: the craft of living, of being fully, vibrantly human, inquiring, thoughtful, responsive, awake—and not least with a fantastic sense of humor that shook life free of rigidities.

When Gurdjieff first explained to young Fritz a fundamental approach to self-knowledge, taught also to adult residents, he wound up his explanation in this way: "Here only teach possibility how become man such as not known in modern times, particularly in Western world." That was the challenge, those were the stakes. The institute was not meant to be an easy place; it was meant to be life-giving, life-changing. Gurdjieff evoked his intention in founding and guiding it as follows: "I wished to create around myself conditions in which a man would be continually reminded of the sense and aim of his existence by an unavoidable friction between his conscience and the automatic manifestations of his nature."

After several immensely fruitful years in the Russian capital cities, the Russian Revolution and civil war disrupted Gurdjieff's efforts to found an institute peacefully and securely for the study of his teaching. He and his closest students were forced to emigrate, taking the long route that many other Russian exiles knew too well—from the Russian heartland to the Caucasus, where they had a good year in Tbilisi before civil war reached it; from the Caucasus to what was then still called Constantinople (now Istanbul), where revolutionary conditions were developing; from there to Germany, but not for long; and finally to Paris, where masses of Russian exiles, from aristocrats now sometimes driving taxis or staffing restaurants to ordinary folk doing their best to scrape by, had found refuge.

Gurdjieff and his immediate circle reached Paris with scant

resources, but the will of fate was not far off. For his part, Ouspensky had already established himself in London as an exponent of the new teaching, whose lectures from week to week were appreciated by people of influence, among them the leading literary editor of that period, A. R. Orage, and a vastly wealthy patroness of intriguing new cultural movements. Through Ouspensky's good will and contacts, sufficient funds reached Gurdjieff in Paris to lease a lovely though neglected property in Fontainebleau-Avon, pupils arrived from England from among Ouspensky's listeners, and the life began that Fritz Peters found his place in, roughly one year after the Institute's founding. The English, and soon after Americans, joined the population of Gurdjieff's students and a core group of Russian exiles to whom Gurdjieff extended a generous hand.

Fritz Peters worked magic in *Boyhood*: he brought the Institute to life. Good books had been published earlier or at the same time, particularly C. S. Nott's *Teachings of Gurdjieff* (1962) and Thomas and Olga de Hartmann's *Our Life with Mr. Gurdjieff* (1964). The de Hartmanns' book is a classic of the Gurdjieff literature, like Ouspensky's *In Search*. But Fritz's book was in a class by itself until the publication decades later of *Gurdjieff: A Master in Life* (2006 in English), a memoir of life at the institute and later by Tcheslaw Tchekhovitch, one of Gurdjieff's earliest pupils and a man whom Fritz would have known. In Tchekhovitch, too, the institute lives again, a tapestry of stories, events, encounters, wisdom at work. Fritz benefited from what you might consider an unfair advantage: the much-adopted boy was in effect adopted by Gurdjieff, who gave him assignments of the most varied kinds, not least the role of personal assistant, bringing him coffee or whatever might be needed at all times of day and night, daily housekeeping in Gurdjieff's personal quarters—all of which offered Fritz access to Gurdjieff and conversations that few if any among the adult residents enjoyed.

The stories and conversations in *Boyhood* are marvels, but it would do you no good to repeat or summarize here: in later pages Fritz will tell us what occurred and what was said in his altogether vivid, inimitable way—often with a Buster Keaton-like, deadpan attitude that left nothing unnoticed. However, I want to highlight two moments in the book and first suggest something about Gurdjieff that strikes me as well worth exploring.

The fundamental Buddhist idea of impermanence has become in today's culture something like a given, a commonly accepted truth. Further, it tends to be met with a degree of sadness, of wistful acknowledgment or consolatory reference to the startling beauty of passing things such as cherry blossoms at a certain moment in the spring. None of this characterizes Gurdjieff's approach. While he put great emphasis on the importance of remembering one's death—the sole means, he thought, of infusing life with seriousness and conscience—he approached changing circumstances with a creative verve that transformed the expected into the unexpected, converted straight-line events into kaleidoscopic wonders. And through this he taught, not through word and idea but through a kind of benevolent stagecraft that caught up all participants and gave them impressions of life and movement and human character—not least, their own. Young Fritz was in the front row, so to speak--he simply loved how Gurdjieff approached life, and later, as a writer, he told us what he had experienced not in Gurdjieff's shadow but in his light. Impermanence was Gurdjieff's medium, a box of colors on which he freely drew. Look for Fritz's story about the soup he prepared that accidentally had a lump of coal in it: that story alone will prove every point made here. Behind and beneath life's changes, as I believe Gurdjieff would say, there was the possibility of an unfailing stability: "I am," a self-aware, vigilant, earned identity.

All was not easy at the institute, far from it. I'll recall just one example. In 1926, Gurdjieff's wife, Julia Osipovna, a woman whom Fritz revered, was close to death from an intractable cancer, and

Gurdjieff was doing all he could for her. In that worst of times, late one night Gurdjieff sat Fritz down and spoke of many things, including this: "You now part of...family—my family—you can help by making strong wish for her, not for long life, but for proper death at right time. Wish can help, is like prayer when for other. When for self, prayer and wish no good, only work good for self. But when wish with heart for other, can help."

Fritz was a recurrent troublemaker—Gurdjieff didn't mind—and just a kid who would forget or strategically overlook assigned duties. Toward the end of his years at the institute, he was made responsible for what he calls the Herb Garden—ennobled by caps—and neglected it to the point that an unidentified adult reported the situation to Gurdjieff, who "made a personal inspection of the garden with me...examining every plant." Difficult! Gurdjieff drew various lessons from the situation for Fritz and led on to an illuminating discussion that I have never forgotten since first reading it. "He talked to me for a very long time that morning, and emphasized the fact that everyone had, usually, a particular, recurring problem in life. He said that these particular problems were usually a form of laziness, and that I was to think about my laziness...not the outward form, which was not important, but to find out what it was. 'When you see that you are lazy, necessary find out what this laziness is. Because in some ways you already lazy for many years, can take even many years for you to find out what it is...This important and very difficult work I give you now.'"

"You not learn my work from talk and book," Gurdjieff remarks to Fritz toward the beginning of *Gurdjieff Remembered*; "—you learn in skin, and you cannot escape. These people (*he indicated others in the room*) must make effort, go to meetings, read book. If you never go to meeting, never read book, you still cannot forget what I put inside you when you child." This retrospect allows us to take leave of *Boyhood* and acknowledge its sequel, yet another powerful book, in which Fritz looks as an adult at the man and teacher who shaped his inner life. There are so many lessons in its pages, such wisdom caught on the fly, and accounts of a number of outrageous situations provoked by Gurdjieff for pedagogic purposes only later understood by Fritz.

When Fritz returned to Gurdjieff in Paris as the war was drawing to a close and Paris was liberated, at first Gurdjieff didn't recognize him. Of course Fritz looked different: he had had a hard war, Gurdjieff hadn't seen him in years, and Gurdjieff was now an old man. "I simply stated my name. He stared at me again for a second, dropped his cane, and cried out in a loud voice, 'My son!'"

ROGER LIPSEY

Roger Lipsey is a biographer, art historian, and translator. He is the author of *Gurdjieff Reconsidered: The Life, the Teachings, the Legacy* (Shambhala Publications, 2019). He received a PhD from the Institute of Fine Arts, New York University.

Fritz Peters at the Prieuré circa 1925

GURDJIEFF

REMEMBERED

Originally Dedicated To:

Victor Gollancz

I

I **HAD SPENT ABOUT FOUR AND** one-half years of my early adolescence as a resident student, in Fontainebleau, France, at Georges Gurdjieff's "Institute for the Harmonious Development of Man," also known as the "Gurdjieff Institute," or, more familiarly, "Le Prieuré," during the years 1924 to 1929. I left there at the age of fifteen to return to Chicago and my family which, at that time, consisted of my mother, Lois, my stepfather, Bill, and a half-sister, Linda, then about seven years old.

My departure had been a difficult one in many ways. For various reasons, mostly because of my mother's long illness, I had been legally adopted by Jane Heap and Margaret Anderson (my mother's sister) and it was through them that I had gone to live at the Gurdjieff school. When I decided to return to America, it became necessary to "break" that adoption, a process which involved considerable legal and personal unpleasantness. My arrival in America was further complicated by the fact that while I was on the ocean the now-famous stock market crash of 1929 came to a head.

Although I had expected that my mother would meet me in New York upon arrival, it did not turn out that way. There was no one at the dock, and I was in the odd position of being a recently "unadopted" minor who was not permitted to leave the ship unless I could be placed in someone's custody. The authorities put me firmly into the hands of an organization known as "The Traveller's Aid Society" whose only solution was to keep me on the ship while they made some attempt to get in touch with my family in Chicago. It was not an auspicious homecoming.

I watched as the ship—the *Leviathan,* at that time the world's largest ocean liner—emptied, and I remained, staring over the railing, like some piece of unclaimed excess baggage. The dilemma was finally solved by the arrival of a man, whose name I no longer remember, who was a business associate of my stepfather and who claimed me in my family's name. He was a pleasant, sympathetic man, but with very little helpful information. He did not know why my mother was not there, but he did know that I was to be given money, put on a train, and despatched to Chicago, all of which he accomplished efficiently so that I found myself on the "Broadway Limited" rattling through the night in the direction of Chicago. I had been, and still was, alarmed at my mother's non-appearance at the ship, but assumed that this would be cleared up upon my arrival in Chicago. It did not turn out to be quite so simple.

There was no familiar face at the Chicago station. Bewildered, I had visions of once more finding myself in the hands of the "Traveller's Aid" and hesitated to ask questions for fear of the resulting "aid." After searching the platform nervously, I was approached by a rather formidable-looking middle-aged woman who asked me my name, and upon learning it, told me that she was there in place of my mother, who was ill. I had, apparently, known this woman as a child but it was some time before my memory was jogged into any recognition of her. When I questioned her about my mother's illness she was merely nervous and vague, and told me that my stepfather, Bill, would explain it all to me when I saw him that evening.

Arriving at our apartment on the south side of the city, I found that there were two people I did remember: my half-sister, Linda, and the coloured woman, Clara, who had been our nurse and housekeeper when I was a very young boy. Even Clara, however, was mysterious about my mother, so I spent the afternoon waiting impatiently for Bill's return from his office and the moment when my questions would be answered.

When he did arrive, about six that evening, the mystery continued. He merely greeted me, with some reserve, and told me that he would "talk to me" later that evening. Then, to my surprise, he mixed a cocktail and asked me if I smoked and drank. I replied, honestly, that while I did not make a habit of either, I had been known to do both. He smiled and offered me a drink and a cigarette, both of which I accepted. He asked me a great many unimportant questions—about my trip across the ocean, etc., but kept the conversation rigorously general. By this time, I had accepted the fact that I would get no information until he chose to give it to me, so I did not press him. However, it did seem a long time before we had finally finished dinner and my sister had been put to bed. I had already understood that she had to be disposed of before he would talk to me.

When we were, at last, alone in the large livingroom of the luxurious apartment overlooking Lake Michigan, Bill's nervousness seemed to increase, and he offered me another drink and a cigarette, which I again accepted. After a great deal of fumbling, hemming, and hawing, he finally sat down facing me, and with a stern expression on his face, produced the document that had been prepared in Paris to dissolve the adoption, a copy of which had been handed to me as I boarded the ship at Cherbourg. I had read it, of course. Not only had I read it and been shocked by it, but I also remembered Jane's words when she had given it to me—on the gangplank of the tender: "You may be shocked when you read this," she had said, "but try to realize my position and remember that it was very difficult to break the adoption without some reason that would be legally valid."

The essence of the document was that I was being "expelled" from the Gurdjieff school because I was "morally unfit." The phrase had no specific meaning for me, at fifteen, and while I had been genuinely shocked and hurt by it, I had taken some meagre comfort from Jane's explanation and, in the course of the trip, had finally assumed that the document had had to be worded that way for, as she had said, "legal reasons" which were beyond my capacity to understand at that age.

How easily do the young place their trust in adults! In addition to that document, I had with me the last letters I had received from Lois and Bill—letters of welcome and glowing descriptions of their preparations for my future. I would be sent to college, I had nothing to worry about now, I had been away too long, it was time I had a good home, and so on...*ad infinitum.* I had already accepted, and believed, these welcoming missives, and my reading of the legal papers had not discouraged me. True, it had worried me, but I counted on the love and trust of my welcoming family, and completely discounted the possible effect of the, to me, meaningless legal phraseology.

Bill, document in hand, corrected my mistaken assumptions in very short order. He began by acknowledging his and Lois's letters, reminding me, however, that they had been written before the document had been received. I said, in all my fifteen-year-old innocence, that I did not see why the "meaningless legal phrases" should alter anything and also quoted to him what Jane had said about it. He thought this over briefly and then said, to my astonishment, that he had thought over the whole question and had come to the conclusion that, since Jane was, as he knew, a difficult person, there was some possibility that she had distorted or exaggerated the facts.

Exaggerated! I asked him what he meant by that and he replied quickly that there must obviously be some truth in the document but that he would like to hear my version of what I had done in order to be expelled. When I said that I did not know what he meant and that, in any case, I had not been expelled, he said that nothing could now be gained by lying.

For his sake, perhaps I had better point out that he was a lawyer and had great respect for legal documents. In any event, after the preliminary conversation, during which we had arrived at some kind of dead-end, he took another tack and asked me if I understood the meaning of the words "morally unfit"? I said that I knew, roughly, that they signified something unpleasant but that they had no precise meaning for me.

He then produced a long letter from Jane which, as he pointed out quite unnecessarily, amplified the meaning of these words. I sat in a kind of frozen horror as he read excerpts from the letter, which, according to him, had been the cause of my mother's hospitalization a few days before, because of a complete nervous collapse. According to the letter, there was very little question but that I was some sort of sexually depraved delinquent given, principally, to the practice of corrupting other, smaller, children. When he had finished reading, I remained silent, and he then poured me another drink and asked me if I realized the problem which now faced him. I shook my head dumbly and said I did not know what he meant, so he amplified his position by pointing out to me that if the allegations in Jane's letter were true, he could not, of course, safely allow me to inhabit this apartment in company with his seven-year-old daughter, my halfsister. With a glance at the drink in my hand, he also mentioned that he did not know of any other fifteen-year-old boys who "smoked and drank."

I then took a deep breath, and a drink, and asked him if he believed that the "allegations" (his word) were true. He said that he was "reserving his opinion" until he had heard my side of the story.

I had been told that the Gurdjieff school was a "preparation for life" of a different, and better, sort than could ever be found in ordinary schools or under ordinary "life conditions." While this may have been true, I did not, at that moment, feel prepared for the problem facing me. After some deliberation (perhaps the preparation had been better than I realized) I said that it seemed to me, in general, that people believed what they wished to believe. I added that, obviously, if I admitted to the "crimes" suggested by the letter, he would believe me. On the other hand, if I denied them, since the charges had been made, he would always wonder if I were telling the truth or not. I said further that since I had no way of proving my "innocence" the only course left to me was to say nothing. That I would leave it up to him—not to decide which one of us, Jane or myself, had been telling the truth—but simply to decide whether or not Jane had been honest. Thwarted and frustrated by this attitude, Bill pressed me for three hours for an affirmation or a denial, but I remained resolutely firm and told him that I was leaving the decision squarely in his hands and on his conscience without any further comments. By midnight, he had decided to continue to "reserve his decision" and told me that, temporarily, I would be allowed to stay in the apartment. He added that he had arranged for someone to take me to visit my mother the following day.

I slept that night, in the library, with a great many misgivings. The world, that night, seemed very large indeed, and equally hostile.

The by now (to me) famous legal document was only the beginning. I did see my mother the next day and, while she greeted me with the kind of affection that was natural to a mother who has not seen her son for a long time, the seed of suspicion had been sown in fertile soil. She was not in the hospital for very long and I was very happy when she came back to live with us, but it also came to mean that I was under double surveillance. I don't know exactly what was expected of me but, looking back, it might have resolved the whole problem had I, as it were obediently, either raped my sister or at least initiated her into some strange and reprehensible sexual practices. The fact that I did not, instead of clearing my name, only prolonged the suspense.

To add to this, I received—in the course of three or four weeks after my arrival in Chicago—several letters from people who had been mutual friends of Jane and of my family and, therefore, of mine. Jane's "coverage" of the events leading up to my return to America had been as complete as possible—as if she had been a onewoman "Associated Press." The content of all these letters was more or less identical. The writer, having heard from Jane, was sorry to hear of my progress in delinquency and felt that it would be better, for all concerned, if I would not make any attempt to get in touch with them.

Having, by this time, resigned myself to the obvious "hostility" of the adult world, I did not express very much feeling when I received these letters. I sensed, somehow, that any sort of protest would be useless and that my only ally—if I had one—was time.

In the meantime, certain definite decisions and arrangements had to be made that related to my future. Largely because of the stock market crash (although we seemed to me affluent enough), it was decided that the idea of my going to college was out of the question. However, I would at least have to have a respectable high school diploma. I was enrolled in high school as a senior, in spite of my previous lack of any acceptable or accredited high school training; apparently certain tests were enough to accomplish this. However, after completing less than one semester (with straight "A's" except in Zoology which I loathed and did not pass) it was decided that I could get along without any further formal education—or any diploma—and Bill's solution was to offer me a job in his law office—I was to be paid $12.00 per week and would have to pay for my own transportation and my laundry; food would be "thrown in" without further expense to me.

After I had been working, presumably satisfactorily, for a few months, my mother told me that she had to talk to me about an important decision she would have to make. She found that she could no longer bear life with Bill and had decided to either divorce him or, at least, separate from him legally. I was sixteen at that time and the recent events of my life seemed to have come full circle, to a total stop. By the fall of that year, 1930, events had followed events rigorously. After a separation and the beginning of a suit for divorce, I found myself living alone on $15.00 a week (I had been given a $3.00 a week raise), still working in my stepfather's office. My mother and my half-sister had fled to Europe and when Bill, who had also made a separate trip to Europe, on business, returned and found them absent, I found myself out of a job.

So, by September of 1930, all the threads had been cut. I was then living alone, without a job, on the accumulated savings from my small weekly salary.

What does all this have to do with Georges Gurdjieff, any reader may well ask. In a sense, nothing; except that, having trusted and perhaps worshipped him for about five years, my feelings for and about him were now strongly reinforced. No one else in the world, or in my experience of the world, seemed willing to give me "house-room" and while the knowledge of his existence was a distant comfort to me, he was somewhere in France, about four thousand miles from Chicago.

II

DURING THE PERIOD 1930 TO 1932, I lived a rather solitary existence. I had found a job as a combination file-clerk and French translator, and was able to live on my small weekly salary.

It was in the fall of 1931 that I came into contact with a group of
about twenty-five people who constituted the so-called "Chicago
Gurdjieff Group." Although I came to know most of them personally
and attended their "group meetings," I found it difficult to understand
their interest in Gurdjieff. They seemed to me to have been attracted
to his teaching for a variety of not very good reasons—because of
loneliness, or perhaps because they considered themselves misfits or
outcasts. Most of them had dabbled in the arts, theosophy, the occult,
or something of the sort, and had come to Gurdjieff as if in search of
another "cure" for their life problems of whatever nature. Gurdjieffian
theory—whatever it might be—seemed acceptable to them precisely
because it was difficult to define. While Gurdjieff himself had always
made sense to me as an individual, I had not had much contact with his
"theories" when I had been at the Prieuré. These theories, as presented
and discussed by this Chicago group were a total mystery to me. I began
to sense a certain danger in his teaching when it was carried on without
his personal supervision.

My more or less unconscious exposure to Gurdjieff's ideas while I
was at the Prieuré had given me some ideas of my own. I thought of

his teaching as something that was intended to stimulate interest in personal self-development, but certainly not as a philosophy that had any bearing on—or interest in—the everyday problems of people. It did not pretend to answer questions or offer solutions to existing difficulties, but (or so it seemed to me) suggested the possibility of a new way of life; a way of acquiring new values and a new morality. How this was accomplished was another question—and I had learned not to ask about that.

The meetings in Chicago, generally, consisted of readings of Gurdjieff's first book which purported to be, in his own words, "an objective, impartial criticism of the life of man," and these readings were usually followed by a discussion period during which these followers seemed to me to attempt to relate his writings to their own individuality. Since the writings were obviously critical of ordinary values, standards and social morality, the group members usually interpreted these criticisms as meaning that any values which ran counter to the prevailing morality were worthwhile. With this view of life, such things as free love, adultery, or any radical social behaviour became almost automatically justified. In other words, while Gurdjieff seemed to me to offer a means of acquiring a new point of view towards life, through work and personal struggles, the prevailing attitude of this particular group of followers was that of substituting new values for old by rote, without any consideration of the means; no attempt was made to acquire—through conscious effort—a new perspective. They behaved as if it were possible simply to decide that they had, overnight, acquired them in their sleep; much as if they had, without any effort whatsoever, suddenly ceased to need to smoke cigarettes.

One of the major differences—for me—between this group and the adults who had, presumably, been involved in the same sort of "work" at the Prieuré, was that these people were all Americans and most of them had never been to the Prieuré. The strictly "American" nature of the group was impressed upon me through the question of morality.

Europeans—at least the Europeans I had known in France and at the Prieuré—appeared to think of "morality" as a code of behaviour covering general human activity including, among a great many other things, sexual activity. To these Americans—or for that matter most other Americans with whom I had any contact—"morality" was confined to sexual codes, and extended perhaps as far as table manners. But no further. Having had, up to that point in my life, no sexual experience, I was both surprised by, and unprepared for, this kind of morality. It came as a distinct surprise to me, therefore, to learn that a good deal of the interest in Gurdjieff seemed to be based on the assumption that life at the Prieuré must have been indiscriminately "free," meaning "licentious." I knew, of course, that Gurdjieff himself was the father of some illegitimate children. I also knew, however, that Gurdjieff (contrary to the opinions of these, and other, people) quite frankly imposed restrictions upon his "disciples" that he did not impose upon himself. He would have been the first person to tell you that he was "extraordinary"—in the sense that he was not bound by average behavioural rules. Once I had begun to comprehend this "American morality" I understood why much of the discussion, following the book readings, was concerned with such questions as free love, etc. The book itself did not, in my opinion, even go into such subjects, but it did lend itself to interpretation of all kinds.

Although these readings left me almost completely in the dark—for the simple reason that it was a difficult book to read and required complete attention and concentration on the part of the reader or listener—there was enough comprehensible material in it to hold my interest and to make me begin to think about the man and his work in a different way than I had before. When the book is read as a straightforward criticism of man's history on the planet Earth, it can have a stimulating, thought-provoking effect and I doubt that this first book was intended as anything more than a critique. In general, although it suggests that there are solutions to the "human dilemma" it does not actually do much more in that direction than to further suggest that there are means which lead to solutions—no actual solutions or answers are given. So much of the criticism in the book is new or radical that it was difficult, if not impossible, to argue against it. In order to retain an interest in the Gurdjieff work one had to accept his view of life, in the same sense that it would, I assume, be necessary to have faith in order to become a genuine, honest follower of, say, the Catholic religion.

The group members, generally, managed to avoid the dilemma of this "faith" or "commitment" by the rather simple expedient of deciding that the Gurdjieff writings were primarily allegorical and, therefore, subject to whatever interpretation they chose to give them. It was rather like getting married without benefit of a licence or a ceremony. I was still young enough to read such a simple statement as the fact that "constipation was the universal disease, particularly of Americans, because their toilet seats were too comfortable," and accept it as meaning nothing more than what it said. I could understand someone arguing that constipation was not a universal disease, but I could not understand it when some group member asserted that Gurdjieff did not mean constipation in the usual sense, but, rather, something emotional or mental. In fact, while the style in which the book is written seems enormously complicated—at least on first reading—the complexity seems to me to be an attempt at absolute precision and calculated to avoid the possibility of any interpretation or "double meaning." When the book states that man, as such, does not have a soul but only has the rather faint possibility of acquiring one, I think the statement is literal, and I further assume that Gurdjieff's assertion that in order to acquire a soul it would be necessary to work, preferably with Gurdjieff, towards this aim, means quite simply what it says. I do not, of course, mean that any reader was compelled to *agree* with such a statement, but I do not feel that it means anything else. I, personally, find the statement acceptable, and am not concerned with whether any other person believes it. My only argument would be with those who assume that it contains a separate, or allegorical, meaning.

Among other things, Gurdjieff, along with accepted religions, seemed to say that one should "love one's enemies," i.e., not have any enemies, and it did not seem to me that such a statement was open to question. The problem, if there was a problem, might lie in the interpretation of the word "love." Gurdjieff's own definition of it—to know enough to be able to help others even when they could not help themselves—was good enough for me and had only one meaning.

By and large, the Chicago "group" fitted in with other Gurdjieff "disciples" I had known—people who were content to take on certain ritualistic, physical attitudes which lacked any inner content. After a short period of association with Gurdjieff and exposure to his writings, people frequently changed the outer expression of themselves and were given to affectations in speech and dress, usually intended to express reverence. One element that was conspicuously lacking in most of Gurdjieff's followers was the one element which he, himself, expressed abundantly—humour. In consequence, the meetings were charged with an atmosphere of grim, humourless, devotion—and a consequent lack of perspective. It seemed to me that if we are as idiotic and unformed as Gurdjieff depicts us to be, it is practically impossible to see ourselves objectively without a sense of the ridiculous. The very posturing and attitudinizing of the group members was evidence of a certain misplaced seriousness. While it was obvious that any solution to the human predicament would involve serious, hard work, the contemplation of ordinary human behaviour was not without its ridiculous aspects. The spectacle of a group of adult, human beings, discussing—in hushed tones—their weaknesses, sins, and general fallibility certainly had its humorous side to me, perhaps particularly because I was one of the group.

III

IT WAS WITH SOME MISGIVINGS that I learned that Mr. Gurdjieff was going to make a visit to Chicago during the winter of 1932. Even now, some thirty years later and with the aid of hindsight, I find it difficult to understand why I did not want to see him. Part of my feeling was unquestionably due to the fact that I had come to believe that I had probably made a mistake when I left the Prieuré in 1929. I felt that I was not, because of my departure, a loyal or faithful follower. In addition, while I had some genuine interest in his writing, and real affection for Gurdjieff as a man, my association with the Chicago group had made me question the validity of his work in all its aspects. I was still looking for some proof—some quality in the behaviour of his followers—that would convince me that he was something more than a powerful human being who was able to mesmerize a good many individuals at will. My interest in his writing was—at that time—nothing more than curiosity concerning his particular speculations and criticisms of mankind. It was not a whole-hearted agreement with his point of view.

I did see him, but not without a good deal of resistance on my part. In fact, if I had not received a message from him asking me to come to see him, I would not have seen him at all. As it was, the meeting was not very satisfactory to me. I went, with a small group of his followers, to meet him at a restaurant in downtown Chicago. It was a noisy place, with music and dancing, and after he had greeted me affection-ately, we proceeded to sit in this din without any further exchange. The other people talked to him incessantly, mostly about uninteresting and, to me, unimportant personal problems, and for a long time my only participation in the proceedings was that he sent me on several errands—to buy cigarettes for him, to buy some special kind of cheese, to telephone some particular group member to come to meet him, etc. Finally, when there was a lull in the general conversation, Gurdjieff turned to me, indicated the couples dancing on the crowded dance floor and asked me if I realized that dancing was a very interesting and almost perfect example of what he called "titillation." I felt that I understood what he meant, i.e., "waste," and said so. He then asked me if I knew that titillation was "social masturbation" which, mostly because of my age, embarrassed me. I managed to say that I agreed with this and he then said that it was time for me to look objectively at the life of people—to observe human manifestations, and to try to understand the difference between genuine, essential, normal human behaviour and "titillation" or "masturbation." He added that while he had used this example of dancing, I should learn to recognize this "masturbation" in other spheres of human activity. As an example, he said that people frequently learned very quickly to turn anything—even their religion and their so-called serious beliefs—into some mean-ingless form of titillation. I made some reference to his statement of many years before that much of mankind was inevitably destined to become nothing more than fertilizer and he was very pleased that I had remembered that conversation. He said, however, that he had been studying the American language recently and had learned many new and useful terms; that he now wanted to change the term "fertilizer" to "shit" because the latter word was a "real" word...an honestly expressive word that gave the proper flavour of that particular human condition. He went on to say that I, like most young people—particularly Ameri-cans—always looked at the world upside down. For example, I assumed that anyone I met was good, honest, upright, etc., etc., and only learned the truth about people though disillusion. This attitude was a long, slow and improper process. "You must learn to look right side up," he said. "Every person you see, including yourself, is shit. You learn this and then when you find something good in such shit people—some possibility not to be shit—you will have two things: you will feel good inside when you learn this person better than you think, and you will also have made proper observation. Just so, when you can observe self, if you already think self is all shit then when see something good in self will be able to recognize at once and will also feel joy. Important that you think about this."

The immediate association in my mind was with the Chicago group members and it did have the effect of changing my attitude about and towards them. Instead of feeling disappointment with them for not manifesting some sort of worthiness because of their association with Gurdjieff's work, I began to look for something else. It did seem a great deal more honest and realistic to look at people, including myself, as worthless—or shit, as he put it—and then discern some small, valid element in them. And, to my surprise, it amounted to a more compassionate view of humanity as well. Instead of watching with a critical eye for signs of failure, I began to watch for signs of success—as one might be delighted when a dog learned a trick—rather than berating it whenever it failed to learn something.

Whether or not this change in my attitude was what Gurdjieff intended is open to question. That was the effect it had on me, and it seems to me that the effectiveness of the Gurdjieff work—or for that matter of any work of that kind—is necessarily determined by the receptivity of the person towards whom it is directed. Be that as it may, that conversation made my future association with the Chicago group, and with people in general, a much less disturbing and much more acceptable process. There was a short period during which the paradox of considering people "shit" and thereby finding myself more in harmony with them, was confusing to me, but I did not puzzle over that for long. I was glad of the change, and that was sufficient.

Our conversation ended that evening with a rather cryptic analysis—by Gurdjieff—of my association with him. Humorously, and apparently relishing some private joke, he said that the other people present were learning his work in a very different way than I had, and that because of my childhood association with him I had certain problems and struggles which they would never experience. "You not wish to come to see me tonight," he said, "so necessary for me—very busy man—to take time to send for you. This because you now have struggle between real self and personality. You not learn my work from talk and book—you learn in skin, and you cannot escape. These people," and he indicated the other group members, "must make effort, go to meetings, read book. If you never go to meeting, never read book, you still cannot forget what I put inside you when you child. These others, if not go to meeting, will forget even existence of Mr. Gurdjieff. But not you. I already in your blood—make your life miserable for ever—but such misery can be good thing for your soul, so even when miserable you must thank your God for suffering I give you."

Before Mr. Gurdjieff left Chicago, I had a private interview with him. I had been puzzled by his remarks about my special problems in relation to his work and had not had any particular desire to pursue the subject further; I was tired of confusion, and his words had only added to my already perplexed state. But, when he asked me to help him cook a meal in his apartment, I did not feel that I could refuse. As it turned out, there was very little work for me to do, and he spent most of our time alone together asking me rather ordinary questions about my family, the work I did, and so on. It was reminiscent of being visited by some old relative who had deigned to take an unexpected interest in some younger member of a family.

When we began to talk about the Chicago group, however, I made a rather impertinent remark about what I called their "phony" attitude towards his work, and particularly towards their so-called morality.

Gurdjieff, who did not usually—in my experience—have any particular taste for opinions or "gossip" about his groups or his disciples, seemed very much interested in my remark and pressed me for details. I went on to say, with a good deal of self-righteousness, that I was leery of his group in Chicago on at least two counts: their phony reverence, as I called it, and their tendency to use his work as an excuse for sexual promiscuity or at least a good deal of talk about sexual promiscuity. Being further prodded by him, I went on about their conception of morality seeming to me to be based almost entirely on sex and not on other customs.

He smiled at this and then said, to my surprise, that he found this completely understandable. "In fact, this is perhaps even good thing you tell me about group people. America is still very young, strong country. Like young people everywhere, all Americans very interested, very preoccupied with sex things. So very natural for them talk and act this way. And not bad thing they do. I tell many times that all work must start with body; like I tell many times that if wish observe self must start from outside, by observing movements of body. Only much later can learn how observe emotional and mental centres. Young people not have very much inside, so not much to observe yet. And this is also good thing, one of reasons I come to America and have many American students. Europeans already blasé, know everything, or think know about philosophy, religion, other such things. This not true. They only have already formed inner self that makes them rotten inside because formed with unconsciousness. Americans more receptive because not closed up inside yet; they naïve, stupid, perhaps, but still real. Americans, particularly, have more chance grow properly as men because have not yet become—like you say—'phony' men. For yourself, I tell always remember look for reasons that eye cannot see. You already notice difference between American and European morality, but when make judgment must observe deeper if wish understand."

I then asked him why it was that I felt so many of his students to be insincere in their interpretations of him and of his work. He asked me to give him an example and I said that they never seemed to me to listen to what he said—that is, the actual words—but that they almost always immediately placed an interpretation on such words which was, to me, manifestly untrue.

"What you say is true," he said, "but if you see this then you must already begin to see how difficult this work. Other evening when I tell that you learn differently from others, I tell truth. When you come Prieuré first time you not yet spoiled, have not learn to lie to self. Already even then you can maybe lie to mother or father, but not to self. So you fortunate. But these people very unfortunate. Like you, when child, they learn lie to parents, but as they grow up also learn lie to self and once learn this is very difficult to change. Lying, like all other things, become habit for them. So when I say even ordinary thing, because they wish have reverence for their teacher—this reverence can be very bad thing, but is necessary for their good feeling—and because also wish not disturb their inside sleep, they find other meaning for what I say."

"In that case," I asked, "how can they ever learn anything from you—or from anyone else?"

"Maybe they not learn anything ever."

"Then why bother to try and teach them?"

He smiled, indulgently. "Because is possibility, even if very small, may learn."

It seemed logical enough, as he put it, but I doubted that there was much in store for most of the people who worked with him.

After leaving his apartment, as I reviewed the conversation, I wondered whether I was making an exception of myself in the sense that I felt I was learning more (or at least *something)* from him than his other students. And I wondered if I was not feeling a little "self-proud" of myself. After turning the questions over in my mind, I could not honestly tell myself that I was in any way particularly vain about my learning. I was proud, in a comparative way, that I had known him personally so much more intimately and for so much longer a time than many of his other students, but as to any actual learning, I could not evaluate it for the very simple reason that if I was learning anything at all from him I didn't know what it was. That did give me a slight clue, but not a very satisfactory one. The clue was simply that if one did acquire knowledge, or learned something from him, it might not necessarily be visible or obvious.

IV

AFTER SEEING MR. GURDJIEFF IN Chicago in 1932, there was an interval of about two years during which I did not see him again. I had moved to New York in the fall of 1933, and one Saturday afternoon when I came home from work my landlord told me that a very strange man, with a heavy, foreign accent had come to see me and wanted me to get in touch with him. The landlord, however, had not been able to understand him, did not know his name, and only knew that whoever he was, he was living at the Henry Hudson Hotel in New York. I thought of Gurdjieff at once, although it was difficult for me to believe that he had gone to the trouble of finding my address and then coming to search for me in person. I went to the hotel immediately and, as I had expected, found him there.

When I got to his apartment in the hotel, he told me that he had tried to find me earlier in the day, but that now it was too late and that he had no further need of—or use for—me. There was no affection in his greeting and he merely looked bored and very tired. In spite of this, and because I was glad to see him and worried about his great weariness, I did not leave but reminded him that he had once told me that "it was never too late to make reparations in life," and that while I was sorry not to have been home earlier, there was surely something I could do now that I had arrived.

He looked at me with a tired smile and said that perhaps there was something I could do. He led me into the kitchen, indicated an enormous pile of dirty dishes and said they needed to be washed; he then pointed to another equally enormous pile of vegetables and said they needed to be prepared for a dinner he was going to give that evening. After showing these to me, he asked me if I had the time to help him. When I had assured him that I did, he told me to wash the dishes first and then prepare the vegetables. Before leaving the kitchen, to rest, he said that he hoped he would be able to count on me to finish both jobs—otherwise he would not be able to rest properly. I told him not to worry and went to work on the dishes. He watched me for a few minutes and then said that several people had promised to help him that day but that there were no members of the New York group who were able to keep their promises. I told him that he had better rest while he had the opportunity and not waste his time talking to me, and he laughed and left the kitchen.

I was finished with my work when he returned and he was very pleased. He then began to cook the evening meal and told me to set the table for fifteen people, adding that some very important people—important for his work—were coming to dinner and that when the food was in the oven he would need me to help him by giving him an English lesson as it was essential that he talk to these people in a certain way—in a language that they would understand correctly.

When we had finished our work, he sat down at the table, told me to sit next to him and then began asking me questions about the English language. It turned out that he wanted to learn, before the guests arrived, all the words for the various parts and functions of the body "that were not in the dictionary." We spent perhaps two hours repeating every four-letter word that I knew, plus every obscene phrase I could think of. By about seven o'clock he felt that he was reasonably proficient with our "slang" vocabulary which he, apparently, needed for his dinner. Inevitably, I began to wonder what sort of people would be coming to dinner. At the conclusion of this "lesson" he told me that it was for that lesson that he had been trying to find me, because I was the first person who, some years before in Chicago, had given him the real flavour and meaning of the words "phony" and "leery"; it seems that these words, in the interim, had become very useful in his conversations with his American students. "These very good words," he said, "raw...like your America."

When the guests did arrive, they turned out to be a group of well-dressed, well-mannered New Yorkers, and, since Gurdjieff had gone to "prepare" himself for dinner, I greeted them and, according to his precise instructions, served them drinks.

He did not appear until most of them had been there for about half an hour, and when he greeted them, he was very apologetic for the delay and extremely effusive about how beautiful the ladies looked and how much they were all honouring him by consenting to be the guests of a poor, humble man like himself. I was actually embarrassed by what seemed to me a very crude form of flattery and by his presentation of himself as an unworthy and very obsequious host. But, to my surprise, it seemed to work. By the time they were seated at the dinner table, all the guests were in a very mellow mood (they had had only one drink so it was not due to liquor) and they began, in a somewhat jocular and superior way, to ask him questions about his work and his reason for coming to America. The general tone of the questions was bored—many of the people present were reporters or journalists—and they behaved as if they were carrying out an assignment to interview some crank. I could already see them making mental notes and could imagine the sort of "funny" interview or feature story they might write. After some questioning by this group, I noticed that Gurdjieff's voice changed in tone, and as I watched him he gave me a sudden, sly wink.

He then proceeded to tell them that since they were all very superior people that they of course knew—since a simple person like himself knew it, then obviously they did—that humanity in general was in a very sad state and could only be considered as having degenerated into real waste matter, or to use a term that was familiar to all of them, pure "shit." That this transformation of humankind into something worthless was especially apparent in America—which was why he had come there to observe it. He went on to say that the main cause of this sad state of affairs was that people—especially Americans—were never motivated by intelligence or good feelings, but only by the needs— usually dirty—of their genital organs, using, of course (as he talked) only the four-letter words which he had practised with me earlier. He indicated one very well-dressed, handsome woman, complimented her on her coiffure, her dress, her perfume, etc., and then said that while she, of course, might not want everyone to know her motives or her desires, he and she could be honest with each other—that her reasons for turning herself out so elaborately were because she had a strong sexual urge (as he put it "wish to fuck") for some particular person and was so tormented by it that she was using every means and every wile she could think of in order to get that person into a bed with her. He said that her urge was particularly, especially strong because she had a very fertile imagination and could already picture herself performing various sexual acts with this man—"such as, how you say in English? 'Sixty-nine'?"—so that, aided by her imagination, she was now at the point where she would do *anything* to achieve her aim. While the company was somewhat startled with this dissertation (not to say "titil-lated"), before anyone had time to react, he began a description of his own sexual abilities and of his highly imaginative mind, and described himself as capable of sustained sexual acts of incredible variety—such as even the lady in question would not be able to imagine.

He then launched into a detailed description of the sexual habits of various races and nations, during the course of which he pointed out that while the French had a world-wide reputation for amorous prowess, it would be well for the people present to make a note of the fact that those highly civilized French used such words as "Mama" and "Mimi" to describe some of their unnatural and perverted sexual practices. He added, however, that in all justice to the French they were, in reality, very moral people and sexually misunderstood and misrepresented.

The guests had all been drinking heavily during dinner—good old Armagnac as always—and after about two hours of unadulterated four-letter word conversation, their behaviour became completely uninhibited. Whether they had all come to believe and accept that they had been invited to an orgy, or for whatever reasons, an orgy—or the beginning of one—was the result. Gurdjieff egged them on by giving them elaborate descriptions of the male and female organs, and of some imaginative uses for them, and finally, most of the guests were physically entangled in groups in various rooms of the apartment, and in various states of undress. The handsome lady had manœuvred herself into a small bar with Gurdjieff and was busily making "passes" of a rather inventive nature, at him.

As for me, I was cornered in the kitchen by an overblown, attractive lady who told me that she was outraged that Gurdjieff should use such words in my presence—I did not look more than about seventeen. I explained, quite honestly, that I had taught them all to him—or at least most of them, and she found this suddenly hilarious and promptly made a pass at me. I backed away and told her that, unfortunately, I had to do the dishes. Rebuffed, she glared at me, called me various dirty names and said that the only reason I had turned her down was because I was "that dirty old man's little faggot," and only wanted him to "screw" me. I was somewhat startled at this, but remembered Gurdjieff's reputation for sexual depravity and made no response.

While the other guests were still hard at it, Gurdjieff suddenly disentangled himself from the lady and told them all, in loud, stentorian tones, that they had already confirmed his observations of the decadence of the Americans and that they need no longer demonstrate for him. He pointed at various individuals, mocked their behaviour and then told them that if they were, thanks to him, now partly conscious of what sort of people they really were, it was an important lesson for them. He said that he deserved to be paid for this lesson and that he would gladly accept cheques and cash from them as they left the apartment. I was not particularly surprised, knowing him and having watched the performance of the evening, to find that he had collected *several thousand dollars*. I was even less surprised when one man told me—as it were, "man to man"—that Gurdjieff, posing as a philosopher, had the best ideas about sex, and the safest "cover" for his orgies, of anyone he had ever known.

When everyone had left, I finished washing the dishes, and to my surprise Gurdjieff came into the kitchen to dry them and put them away. He asked me how I had enjoyed the evening and I said, youthfully and righteously, that I was disgusted. I also told him about my encounter with the lady in the kitchen and her description of my relationship with him. He shrugged his shoulders and said that in such cases the facts were what constituted the truth and that I should never consider or worry about opinions. Then he laughed and gave me a piercing look. "Is fine feeling you have—this disgust," he said. "But now is necessary ask yourself one question. With who you disgusted?"

When I was ready to leave the apartment, he stopped me and referred again to my experience with the lady. "Such lady have in self many homosexual tendencies, one reason she pick on you—young-looking boy, seem almost like girl to her. Not worry about this thing she say to you. Gossip about sex only give reputation for sexiness in your country, so not important, maybe even feather in hat, as you say. Some day you will learn much more about sex, but this you can learn by self, not from me."

V

MR. GURDJIEFF STAYED IN NEW York for several months, through
the winter and spring of 1934, and I saw him regularly. My relationship with him, more or less of its own accord, fell back into a pattern
that resembled our earlier years at the Prieuré. Once again, I became
a sort of functionary of the household, helping to cook, wash dishes,
run errands, etc. I also attended meetings, lectures, and readings but
without much active interest. I was far more involved with the man
himself—as I had been as a child—than with his teaching.

I had planned to go to Chicago during my two weeks' vacation in the
summer of 1934, and when Mr. Gurdjieff learned of this he decided
that he would make a visit to Chicago at the same time as it would be
convenient for him to have me as a travelling companion. I was very
proud to be "selected" to act as his companion and secretary when he
went to Chicago and I looked forward to the trip. For some reason, I
think because he felt it would be a suitable time for him, we were to
leave on a train at midnight. I was packed and ready for the trip early in
the evening and went to his apartment in what I thought was plenty of
time. What with his packing—piles of clothing, books, food, medicine,
etc.,—he was not ready to leave the apartment until well after eleven
p.m., and when we arrived at the station with only about ten minutes
to spare we were met by a large delegation of the New York followers.
It seemed that each one of them had some urgent last-minute business

to take up with him, and about two minutes before train time I interrupted him impatiently, and told him we had to board the train. He said that he had to have a few more minutes—that the extra time was absolutely essential—and for me to talk to someone and arrange to delay the train. I looked at him dumbfounded, but realized that there was no arguing with him. I managed to find some official and made up some story about the importance of Mr. Gurdjieff which, to my great surprise, was effective, and the official agreed to hold the train for ten minutes. Even so, Mr. Gurdjieff did not manage to complete his urgent farewells until the train was actually moving and I had to push him through the door of the last car with his six or seven pieces of luggage. As soon as he was in the moving train, he began to complain in a loud voice about having been interrupted and demanded that a bed be prepared for him immediately. The conductor, with my help, explained to him that our berths were thirteen cars ahead and that we would have to walk to them—very quietly, as most of the other passengers had boarded the train early and were already asleep—through the entire train. Gurdjieff looked appalled, sat down on one of his suitcases, and lighted a cigarette. The conductor or porter told him that smoking was forbidden except in the men's room and he groaned loudly about this hardship, but did consent to put out his cigarette.

It must have taken us—Gurdjieff, conductor, porter, and myself—at least forty-five minutes to get to our assigned berths. Our progress—with all the luggage and with Gurdjieff's lamentations about the rude treatment he was receiving—was so noisy that we awakened almost everyone on the train. In every car, heads would appear through the curtains to hiss at us and curse us. I was furious with him, as well as exhausted, and was greatly relieved when we found our berths. Then, to my horror, he decided that he had to eat, drink and smoke, and began unpacking his bags in search of food and liquor. I was finally able to force him into the men's room. Once in there he settled down to eat and drink and to discourse in loud tones about the terrible service on American trains and the fact that he—a very important man—was being treated in this shoddy fashion. When we were finally threatened—in no uncertain terms—by both the conductor and the porter, with expulsion from the train at the next stop, I lost my temper completely and said that I would be glad to get off the train in order to get away from him. At this, he looked at me in wide-eyed innocence and wanted to know if I was angry with him-and, if so, why. I said that I was furious and that he was making a spectacle of both of us, so he put his food and drink away sadly and then, lighting another cigarette, said that he had never imagined that I, his only friend, would talk to him in this way, and quite literally, desert him. This attitude only increased my anger and I said that once we arrived in Chicago I hoped never to see him again.

He then went to bed in his lower berth, still very sorrowful and still muttering about my unkindness and lack of loyalty, and I climbed into the upper berth hoping for some much-needed sleep. After about five minutes, punctuated by moans and groans from Gurdjieff as he tossed and turned in the lower berth, and by renewed hissing and cursing from the other passengers, he began to talk in a loud voice, complaining that he needed a drink of water, had to have a cigarette, and so forth. There were more threats from the porter and finally, at about four a.m., he settled down and did go to sleep.

We were the last passengers to awaken the next morning and while he dressed and made several trips to the men's room in whatever state of undress he happened to be at the moment, we were stared at by a car full of hostile travelling companions who had, of course, identified us as the troublemakers of the night before. After about one hour, I managed to get him to the dining car, hoping for a peaceful breakfast, but once again my hopes were dashed. There was nothing on the menu that he could eat, and we had long, irritating conversations with the waiter and the head steward about the possibility of procuring yoghurt and similar—at that time—exotic foods, accompanied by vivid descriptions of his particular digestive process and its highly specialized needs. After several long discussions, he suddenly gave in and ate, without any visible discomfort but with a great many complaints, a large American breakfast.

As the train did not arrive in Chicago until late that afternoon, I was not looking forward to spending the day in the Pullman car, but once again I hoped for the best. My fears, however, were well-grounded. I have never, in my life, spent such a day with anyone. He smoked incessantly, in spite of complaints from the passengers and threats from the porter; drank heavily, and produced, at intervals when we seemed momentarily threatened with peace, all kinds of foods, mostly different varieties of strong-smelling cheeses. Although he apologized profusely every time the other passengers complained about his behaviour, he also constantly found new ways to annoy, irritate and offend them—not to mention me.

When we did actually arrive in Chicago it seemed to me nothing less than a miracle. Whatever my opinion of the "Chicago group," when I saw a large number of them on the platform waiting to greet him, I was delighted. I helped him off the train with all his luggage and told him that I was leaving then and there and that he need not expect to see me again. When he heard this, he raised such an outcry on the platform that, for the sake of peace, I consented to go with him and the group members to the apartment they had rented for him. Although I was already furious and outraged, the sight of the fawning disciples made me even more angry. They had prepared, with obvious effort, a "Gurdjieff-type" dinner and they did everything they could think to please him. To my further disgust, he began to praise each one of them individually, telling them what a ghastly trip he had had on the train, how horribly I had treated him, and how different it would have been had only some of them—loyal, devoted, respectful followers—been along to take care of him properly and with the respect that was due to him. I was then promptly assailed by the more ardent members of the group, and attacked for treating their leader with such disrespect, and so on.

After about an hour of this, I reached some sort of breaking-point, and told him and the group I was leaving. Gurdjieff looked at me in amazement and said that he would not be able to stay in Chicago, all alone in such a large apartment, unless I was there with him; that I could not leave him alone under any circumstances. To the horror of the group, I told him that since he was now safely surrounded by a large bunch of the faithful, he could very safely dispense with my services and that I was sure he would find them able and willing to perform any of the services he might require. In the course of this outburst I described some of their possible services in a few of the well-chosen four-letter words that he and I had worked over in New York—and the group members regarded me with disgust as well as with increased horror.

I did not see him again in Chicago, in spite of several messages begging me to take him back to New York, and on my return to New York I carefully avoided him and the New York group until I knew that he had sailed back to France.

VI

THE NEXT TIME I SAW Mr. Gurdjieff—in New York a year or two later—I found that our relationship had changed in many ways. It had taken me several months to calm down after that nightmare journey to Chicago and I came to feel that he had—by his behaviour on that trip—forced me out of the pattern of hero-worship which had unconsciously formed in me in relation to him. I no longer "loved" him in that unquestioning, idealistic way, and I no longer looked back on my early years as I had—filled with pride because of my close relationship to the "master." I saw myself as having been useful in many very ordinary ways to a man who could always put people to use if they happened to be around him. At the next encounter with him, I greeted him more as a kind of equal, although not without a feeling of genuine respect, and I left the work of serving, dishwashing and running errands, to other, more abject, members of the group. He made no objection to my new attitude and seemed content to treat me as a companion rather than a body-slave.

I must admit, however, that when we first met again—this time he was staying at the Great Northern Hotel—I came very close to falling back into the old pattern almost at once. Not only did he look weary and much older, but the atmosphere of the room—with milk cartons on the window-sill, and general disorder in the two small rooms—was shoddy. He sighed and groaned, complaining about the lack of interest and enthusiasm on the part of his so-called followers, and the fact that he had no money and was forced to earn it, in addition to attending lectures, readings, dance groups, etc. My immediate, natural response was to want to help him out in some way, but I managed to resist it this time. I did, however, go to see him (he had complained among other things, of being lonely) and in the course of some of these visits, I learned at first hand about some of the ways in which he "earned money" when it was not forthcoming in the nature of contributions from the disciples. I became acquainted with a stream of "patients"—at least they were not the usual "followers"—who came to him regularly for "treatments" of various kinds. Most of them were afflicted with something: they were alcoholics, dope addicts, just plain neurotics, homosexuals, and what could be called "adult delinquents" of one kind or another. I gathered that they paid him well to "cure" them of whatever disease or manifestation happened to be afflicting them. I do not know in what the cures consisted, except that all of them required long and frequent visits with him at all hours of the day or night—in fact, whenever he could spare the time. Whatever means were used, the effect on the individuals was the usual one: they worshipped him, at least temporarily. The difference between them and the "group" members, was that in their case the worship was, if possible, even more personal and had nothing to do with his ideas or his "method." And this was combined, in most cases, with gratitude for the "cures."

This period of having to earn money did not last very long, and it was a relief to me when it was over. I had not enjoyed my visits to Gurdjieff at that time, and I was glad when he emerged from this rather woebegone characterization of a kind of quack-doctor living in shoddy circumstances. I can only assume that he was able to earn enough money—and perhaps cure enough people—to give up what had never seemed much more than an impersonation to me. The derelicts also vanished from the scene.

From that time on, when I did go to see him, I went to the Childs' restaurants, which he referred to as his "office," and where he liked to sit and do his writing, and I also made a few short boat trips with him—usually to New Jersey.

On one of those trips, when he was once more accompanied by several of "the faithful" (as I had now come to call the disciples) he introduced me to a man and a woman who were not, as he pointed out carefully, married. He said that the man liked to marry women and had been married and divorced several times, but that he had not yet married this woman—that he was, as it were, trying her out—and that, therefore, she was his "handkerchief." He went on to give a long dissertation on the relations between the sexes. He said that there was something—a kind of relationship that rarely existed in modern times—that was worthy of the term "real marriage"; that marriage as we knew it was nothing more than legal sexual intercourse, and that since most people, men and women, were sexually motivated and therefore needed variety, such relationships rarely lasted and usually ended in divorce. He said that there were occasional exceptions to this rule—when a deeper, more valid relationship developed out of something that was purely sexual in the beginning, but that this was rare. Most relationships, whether legal or not, were merely that of man and "handkerchief," as witness this particular couple. "For him," he said, "this very convenient; he suddenly feel need or wish to blow nose—and always he have this handkerchief with him. And after blow nose, not necessary carry such excretion in pocket. This 'woman-handkerchief' can walk all by self. Very, very convenient for modern man. Especially convenient for this man because for him necessary blow nose very often; is his favourite diversion."

He smiled at the two of them after this description, and they smiled back at him. Once again, I was astonished at the way in which people accepted these pronouncements. Not that I expected protests of outrage, but this meek agreement always surprised me. And agreement alone was not enough—usually they would manage to make some interpretation of just such a description of themselves that would turn out to be flattering to them, and would even go so far as to repeat their version of his comments—with, of course, their flattering interpretation—to other group members.

This conversation occupied us for most of the trip and when we arrived at the house of some friends of his in New Jersey, he insisted that they take us to a local market where he bought several pounds of garlic which he said he required for the preparation of some special dish that he wanted to make. When we had made the purchase, we returned to our hosts' house and he instructed everyone—seven or eight of us had come with him—to start peeling and otherwise preparing this mass of garlic. While I did not refuse outright to help with this chore, I simply did not participate, but sat with him on the terrace of the house and drank a good deal of Applejack, which he had only recently discovered. After some time had passed he suddenly asked me, pointedly, how it happened that I was not helping to clean garlic. I answered that I had not made the trip in order to clean garlic—that I simply did not want to help. He then asked me if I thought that I was in some way privileged, and I said, baiting him, that I did not really consider myself worthy of such important work. He poured us each another glass of Applejack and said that I would never be able to realize what trouble he had with his students. No matter how hard he worked with them, just when they reached a stage where he thought he could rely on them, they turned out to be unreliable, etc. He added that I was a good example, a case in point. He had spent years, involving an amount of effort that I could not even imagine, training me to be a worthy, reliable follower, and that now, just when it was important for me to help with the cleaning of the garlic, I was failing him. I said that if I had learned anything from him it was that one could not rely on others—particularly for such important tasks as garlic-cleaning.

He berated me for my irreverent manner of talking to him and then suddenly switched the conversation. He told me that it was a great satisfaction—personally—to him to watch a group of his devoted followers faithfully performing a task which he had assigned to them. We paused to look at the six or seven industrious followers working with the garlic, and I said, pouring another glass of Applejack for each of us, that I could easily understand his pleasure and that, for the time being, I was content to sit with him and share that particular joy. He then cursed me again for my lack of seriousness, but even so he laughed and we continued to drink together. After a fairly long silence, he suddenly asked me why I had not been coming regularly to the group meetings, readings, etc., and I said that I did not feel that I qualified, by my attitude—or in my heart—as a proper follower; that I disagreed with the general feeling of worship that was accorded to him by most of the New York group—or any group—and was uncomfortable in their atmosphere.

When I had said this, he looked at me quite seriously, and said: "You remember I tell you that what I teach is in your blood; that you cannot forget, no matter how you try?"

I said I did, and he said: "What you just tell me is proof of just this teaching. Group work is important, when people work together they can help each other, can make work easier; but since you have not right feeling with group you now make, unconsciously, difficulties and suffering for yourself. Just because of what I teach you in past you now make extra struggles for yourself. This can be good for your future, but also very difficult. You poisoned for life."

He did not say any more and we continued to drink in silence until all the garlic was ready. He then told them to soak it in some sort of solution—in a barrel—and that he would return at some future date to finish the concoction. I, at least, never heard of the garlic again.

VII

AFTER MANY VISITS TO THE United States, over a period of more than ten years, Gurdjieff had become known to a rather large group of people, particularly in New York City. Perhaps inevitably, as some knowledge of his work filtered down by word of mouth to a larger public, he began to acquire a series of reputations. In addition to being known as a serious philosopher and mystic, he also became "famous" or "infamous" for being a charlatan, a quack, a faith healer, etc. As a result of these reputations, and also because of certain misconceptions about him and his work, he began to be sought out and visited by people from all walks of life for a variety of reasons that had little to do with his primary aim. As has been pointed out, he brought a good deal of this upon himself during certain periods, such as the times when—for money—he performed "cures" for some people, or at least gave them some kind of treatments.

While I have often thought that some of these encounters or meetings could have been—and might better have been—avoided, it is difficult and perhaps unfair to attempt to assess his reasons for allowing himself to become involved with so many different people. At the time it seemed simple enough to speculate on the subject and I remember having felt that he was, in a sense, trapped by his own unquestionably genuine interest in people and his equally genuine desire to help anyone who was in any sort of trouble. He was, on the one hand, an easy target.

But, given his complex nature, he unquestionably also amused himself with a good many of the "games" he played with people.

Most of those who came to him were, undoubtedly, in some sort of trouble and they were frequently sent to him by well-wishing members of any one of the American "groups." In almost all cases, the "trouble" was of a psychosomatic nature, and the results of his advice were not always salutary, due, largely, to the lack of complete co-operation on the part of the suppliants.

In one instance, a group of well-wishers petitioned him to come to the aid of a woman in her early fifties who, after having been—at least supposedly—a semialcoholic for several years, had sought the advice of a medical doctor for some ailment that did not pertain directly to her "alcoholism," and part of her doctor's treatment had been to forbid her to drink alcohol in any form. Gurdjieff said that it would be necessary for him to see the woman before he could possibly consider doing anything for her, and after he had seen her and questioned her he said that there was nothing basically wrong with her except that she was going through a period of chemical imbalance which was perfectly normal for a woman of her age. He added, however, that her intake of alcohol over a period of years was in no sense alcoholism and that, in fact, she had an endemic need for a certain amount of alcohol and that to discontinue drinking entirely could be very serious—even fatal; he even prescribed the amount she was to take daily and said that except for certain perfectly normal symptoms that had to do with change-of-life and would not last for a very long time, she was—as long as she continued to drink the amount prescribed—perfectly healthy. He added that it was important for several reasons that his advice be followed and that it should not be disclosed to the doctor. He also said that he wanted to see her from time to time and that, eventually, her need for alcohol would gradually diminish of itself but that he would want to supervise the process. As to his reasons for not telling the doctor about his advice, he said that doctors, in general, did not like to have their patients consult other doctors "behind their back" and to have them consult someone like himself, who was not a legally recognized physician, would make it inevitable that any doctor would immediately repudiate his advice and his prescriptions.

The woman in question was, of course, delighted with his advice and showed immediate improvement, which, as Gurdjieff pointed out, was largely due to the fact that he had, essentially, agreed with her own diagnosis of herself. He added that this was not always the case, of course, but that this particular woman was, generally, "very much in tune with her own system" and he urged her to follow her own instincts when she manifested any form of illness and not to consult physicians except in emergencies or because of accidents which had nothing to do with her fundamental physical condition.

The woman remained in good health for many months, until a misguided well-wishing friend of hers, anxious to interest the doctor in Gurdjieff and to prove that Gurdjieff was, in most respects, a better doctor than the physician in question, told him that the woman's improvement was due entirely to following Gurdjieff's advice which had been the exact opposite of his. The doctor, reacting as Gurdjieff had predicted, convinced the woman that she was slowly poisoning herself with alcohol and promptly had her hospitalized—having managed to convince her somehow that Gurdjieff was, in reality, a quack—with strict instructions against the consumption of any form of alcohol and, in a very sharp period of time, the woman was dead.

Gurdjieff was very distressed on learning of her death and said that while it was true that the woman had been "very much in tune" with her physical self, she had not been a very intelligent or courageous person and that she had not had the basic moral strength to resist trusting— and continuing to consult—a recognized "physician-doctor." He also said that this was a very good example of what would inevitably happen when people consulted him and followed his advice—frequently radical—but did not, at the same time, manage to trust him completely.

A similar case involved a woman who was slowly dying in a hospital, to the great distress of her friends. Gurdjieff was persuaded to visit her and after seeing her said, although not to the woman herself, that her illness was not physical but that she had a strong desire to die—a death-wish as we would undoubtedly phrase it—and that she needed to have something to believe in and live for, as well as some immediate physical treatment. He managed, apparently, to convince her that there were reasons to continue her existence, and his treatment was to prescribe daily olive-oil enemas which were to be taken without the knowledge of her doctors. (She was able to do this by using a small baby-size syringe and having small amounts of olive oil brought to her.) He said that the reason for this prescription was that she had a condition which he described as a kind of long-term constipation due to her nervous and emotional state and that her intestines were coated with hard, dried waste matter which the olive oil would gradually break down, dissolve and eliminate.

The woman was enthusiastic, mainly because of Gurdjieff's interest in her, and the treatment worked and her condition improved rapidly. When, because of the woman's boasting about Gurdjieff's medical abilities, the doctors learned of his advice, the treatment was immediately discontinued. This time, however, the woman lived. But, when she was out of the hospital she was vituperative against Gurdjieff because he had "caused trouble for her with her doctors." Gurdjieff was amused by this and stated that she had achieved what he knew she needed—she now had a good reason to live—active hatred, with himself as the temporary target.

While there was a good deal of discussion—pro and con—among the group members, and others who knew about Gurdjieff, concerning these two cases, neither of them caused him any trouble with either the doctors or the authorities.

There was, however, one case that did cause him considerable trouble and which, eventually, made it difficult for him to stay in the United

States or to re-enter once he had left. This case, like the others, involved a woman. As I remember it, the woman—quite young—met him in Chicago and, in addition to her interest in his ideas, became greatly attracted to him physically. He discussed her case at one time in my presence and said that she was an unfortunate victim of modern society in that she was not generally accepted by other people because she was physically unattractive, found difficulty in communicating with others, and had certain unpleasant manifestations which, although due primarily to her innate shyness, were displeasing to other people. He said that it was natural enough that she should "fall in love" with a man like himself who had treated her with kindness and consideration. He also said that while it would be difficult, if he were able to work with her personally for a few months, he would be able to do a great deal for her and that she would automatically grow out of her infatuation with him.

One major difficulty in this suggested programme was that the young woman's family considered her a semi-invalid and was very much opposed to her having any sort of association with Gurdjieff. In spite of this, the young woman managed to break away from her parents and follow Gurdjieff to New York where she began to see him regularly and to follow him about like a lost lamb.

For a time, she was an object of ridicule to many members of the New York group and there was considerable loose speculation about the nature of her association with Gurdjieff; many people, even among his so-called followers, seeming only too glad to seize on any exceptional association of Gurdjieff's as a proper topic for gossip and speculation. He once spoke of this to me and said that it was the rather sad, but usually unavoidable, reaction of people against anyone they professed to admire.

While I know nothing about the nature of this woman's association with Gurdjieff, I do know that it was suddenly and rudely interrupted by the appearance of some members of the young woman's family who proceeded to accuse Gurdjieff of having "immoral sexual relations" with her and followed up the accusation by having her locked up in a mental institution.

Up to this point, particularly since there was no proof to substantiate the accusations, things were not too serious, although a good many of us were worried about possible difficulties for Gurdjieff for "practising medicine without a licence" and because of his status as a visiting alien in the United States.

When the despondent young woman took her own life after a week of incarceration, however, the picture became very black. Because of renewed charges against Gurdjieff—fanned, oddly enough, by the ardent feelings of some of his supposed followers—he was put in custody on, I believe, Ellis Island for a period of about ten days. During that time, I heard every known charge against him as well as a great storm of gossip and speculation, and also all the arguments of an opposing faction who had dedicated themselves to the cause of clearing his name. This latter group did, finally, prevail by using various kinds of pressure but his name was never, as far as I know, completely cleared and the incident remained a black mark against him. As a result, his stay in America was curtailed and he left a divided group behind him in New York.

Many years later, he referred to this episode and said that it had had one extremely meritorious result in that it had served as a shock which had separated "the wheat from the chaff" of his American adherents.

VIII

DURING ONE OF MR. GURDJIEFF'S many visits to America, I remember that he spent a great deal of time going to the movies. He said that one great difficulty for him in the western world was, that being of a basically eastern temperament and nature, it was often hard for him to comprehend the underlying western mentality. He said that while most westerners would assert that the movies were an exaggerated conception of American life and did not present a true picture of America, he disagreed. He did agree that the active physical behaviour represented in the movies was exaggerated; however, he claimed that the underlying motives—and the hopes, dreams, and desires of Americans in general—were very accurately portrayed in films. In fact, he said that only in the movies was the prevalent American attitude towards sex, for example, revealed for what it really was. He went on to say that his statements could not, in any case, be challenged because the mentality of movie producers was obviously such that they could not invent anything but could only copy—and occasionally distort—life, which is, according to him, exactly what they did.

When he expanded on the subject of sex, in or out of the movies, he said that it was perfectly obvious that while the function of sex had originally only been to ensure the reproduction and continuation of the human race, it had become something very different since it had been "civilized" in America and elsewhere in the western world. He said that sex, being basically the source of all energy and therefore, potentially, the well-spring, for example, of art, had also become for most people nothing more than the most titillating diversion of the many forms of amusement known to modern man. Because of this, energy that could be used—and was destined to be used—for a serious, and high purpose, was simply wasted; thrown away in a frantic chase after pleasure. While he did not specifically condemn this activity any more than he condemned other ordinary, civilized habits, he criticized it from the point of view that any waste is improper to man.

He suggested that human needs, generally, had not been subject to the same kind of "perversion" as in the case of sex. The drives to eat, to eliminate waste matter from the body, to sleep, etc., were, in their own ways, equally strong. In fact, if a given individual had a sufficiently strong need to go to the bathroom—or was dying of thirst or hunger—no amount of sexual provocation could possibly come before any one of these needs. The pleasure involved in drinking water when really thirsty was, of course, different from the gratification of a sexual need, but equally compelling. He pointed out that this perversion of sex was a question that could be profitably studied and examined by everyone and that any diversion of the sexual impulse into more creative channels than sheer satisfaction could be a worthwhile task for anyone.

When people questioned him, as they often did, about specific sexual "perversion" he waved away their questions as hair-splitting. Perversion was perversion, no matter what particular form it might take—there was no question of "good perversions" or "bad perversions"—sex, generally, was perverted when it served to perform anything other than the basic intentions of nature: to produce children and to produce energy which was to be used for higher aims, certainly, than mere physical or emotional gratification. When improperly used such energy was always harmful.

Gurdjieff frequently used sex as a kind of shockfactor in dealing with individuals. I remember the case of one young woman, a dancer, whose principal attraction to Gurdjieff's work was that she was allowed to teach his dances to newcomers because she was a good dancer and a reasonably good teacher. Her interest in his work did not, however, seem to go beyond this pleasure in having a position of some authority. When she once challenged some statement he had made during the course of a lecture, he told her that he would have to give her a personal answer to the questions she was raising and would arrange for someone to give her a definite appointment to see him alone.

That night, after the lecture, he told me to go to her and invite her to come to his room at three o'clock in the morning—alone. He also told me to tell her that he would show her some wonderful things—things that she could not even imagine. When I gave her the message, she listened scornfully and with a show of a good deal of righteous shock and anger told me to tell him that she recognized a "proposition" when she heard one and that not only would she not come to his room but that she would no longer have anything to do with his work.

He was very amused when I relayed this reply to him and said that she had made an unfortunate, for her, but good, for him, choice. He said that her preoccupation with sex was such that she was no longer a good teacher of his dances and that he had chosen this means— face-saving for her—of dismissing her as a teacher. He added, however, that there were times when he was not above "diverting" himself in the current American fashion and that they might both have been rewarded had she agreed to visit him. Then he went on to say that it was just as well since he did not really have the time to deal with the rever- berations that would undoubtedly have followed had she accepted his "proposition." He also said that her refusal would serve her as a topic of conversation and imaginative thought for the rest of her life. On the one hand, she could say that she had "rejected" the great Gurdjieff's advances, and on the other hand she could spend her life wondering what it would have been like had she accepted. I remember the reaction of one female group member on learning—from the dancer herself, of course, who lost no time in spreading the story—of the incident. With a pained look on her face, she said to me: "If it had only been me! What an opportunity! Can't you get me an appointment?" I suggested that she might approach him directly and let him know of her availability but, again sadly, she had to admit that she "didn't have the nerve."

It also seemed to amuse Gurdjieff to describe, always in accurate detail, the sex lives or the sexual history of some of the people who came to him for advice. He said that since sex, by its nature, only permitted of a rather limited repertory, it was simple to deduce the particular forms of satisfaction which were attractive to certain natures or temperaments. The descriptions were invariably vulgar and often amusing.

I have heard a great many stories and a great deal of gossip about Gurdjieff's own reputed sexual practices, most of which were obviously untrue and seemed to stem from the fact that anyone who has set himself up as a leader, or who has a "school" of an unusual nature, must also, more or less automatically, have an unusual and varied sex life. The only somewhat unusual truth about this aspect of his life that I know to be a fact is that he did have children by a few different women to whom he was not married; a normal, if not legal, performance, and a far cry from the practices, rites, and orgies which I have heard ascribed to him.

Even now, many years after his death, I find that it is not uncommon for people who know of him by reputation to inquire about his sexual practices, often suggesting that they must have been not only very interesting and unusual (and, incidentally, that I had certainly either participated in them or at least knew all about them), but even a part of his teaching; they are always disappointed—one might say even disillusioned—to learn the opposite, particularly to learn that he was married, reacting almost as if that was the final sin for anyone of his "peculiar" stature.

IX

IN SPEAKING OF CONTEMPORARY AMERICA, Gurdjieff sometimes made reference to the "new American Gods," the scientists,
and more particularly the personal gods—doctors and psychiatrists. He seemed to feel that doctors were a dangerous breed for,
even though they were often motivated by high-sounding principles
such as a dedication to saving the lives of people, they knew very
little about humanity, almost nothing about the inter-relation of
the mind, the emotions, and the body, and that their aim was not,
generally, to aid or save people, but simply to eradicate disease. He
said that man was not only the chief, but perhaps the only, organism
that interfered constantly and radically with the balance of nature,
a very dangerous activity under any circumstances, and particularly
dangerous when men did not know what they were doing and did
not even take nature into consideration. He said that nature was in-
finitely patient, constantly adapting herself to the strains imposed
on her by these machinations of mankind, especially scientists, but
he warned that nature would, in the long run, be forced to "get
even," as it were, and impose a proper balance and harmony on man.

As to doctors and disease, it would not be correct to say that he was an
advocate of euthanasia or that he thought that the prevention of disease
was a bad aim; but there is no question but that the prolongation of
human life, under any and all circumstances and at any cost, was, in his

opinion, useless and, objectively, immoral. Each life had, according to him, a purpose and rhythm of its own, and it was only our abnormal fear of death and the fact that we seemed to regard it as not only fearful but even evil, that forced us to attempt to prolong physical life at any cost. It was especially valueless since life, as we knew it, had little value or conscious purpose even for those who were completely healthy, physically, and in no way threatened by disease or death. He was interested in the statistics concerning major diseases—the primary killers—and said that the prevalence of heart disease and cancer, for example, was proper to the kind of civilization we had produced and in which we had to live. These two "diseases" along with lesser, non-fatal ailments, such as ulcers, were almost always the inevitable results of living in an unharmonious atmosphere under constant strain and pressure.

Many of Gurdjieff's adherents were depressed by his often-repeated, flat statement that human beings could really learn and could still "change" only until they reached the age—usually in their early twenties—of a certain kind of maturity: the moment when they ceased to grow automatically. Once that point had been reached, life was nothing more than a kind of running-down process, like the unwinding of a spring, and nothing new could be absorbed or learned. As many people had come to him long after reaching this "maturity," they were not only depressed by this theory but, usually, managed to interpret it to mean something entirely different—anything that would make it possible for them to have continued hope and feelings of encouragement.

At one time, I commented on the fact that I had seen people at the Prieuré, in various groups, and now again in New York, who seemed to me to interpret his ideas in such a way as to give themselves hope and a "good feeling" and often managed, by such interpretations, to avoid the simple truth or fact that he was stating. He said that it was important not to be hard on people, that one could not begrudge them hope and that if by this means they were able to continue with his teaching they might, somehow, absorb something of value—if not for this life—then for the next. He also said that this tendency to "interpret"—to make his theories more "digestible"—was an indication of how greatly people felt a need for reassurance, direction, or learning of some kind, and that it was a need that should not be despised. He also said that while one individual might be able to influence, in small ways, a great many other individuals, in the final sense one man could only pass on the knowledge he had acquired to one other man, which was one of the great trials of teachers throughout history. He also said that as one grew and learned in life one came to know that one's own suffering was as nothing when compared with the necessity of having to watch the seemingly unnecessary suffering of others. In a sense, he said that the hardest trial of life was the inability to alleviate the suffering of others—and what made it worse was that most human suffering was valueless in that it never served a useful purpose—was never experienced consciously, for a proper aim. Instead of "using" their suffering for the development of their higher consciousness, people spent all their time using every means they could find in an attempt to alleviate suffering that, in any case, could not be alleviated. He further said—and repeated it in his writings—that if individual men could ever learn to live with the constant knowledge and consciousness of the inevitability of their own, personal death, they would already have achieved a great deal in the way of growth and of preparing themselves for real learning. But the sad fact, according to him, was that the state of our consciousness, generally, was such that this realization was actually impossible. In certain states, to which men are subject, it was possible for them to long for death and an end to human life struggles, but this was a very different thing from the conscious acceptance of the implacable, undeniable, inevitability of death for *oneself*. It was possible to envision the death of others, even those to whom one was greatly attached, but never our own.

During that period in New York, I remember feeling strongly that while Gurdjieff, in an outer sense, seemed to me a prophet of doom and disaster and hopelessness, he nevertheless gave an effect of great encouragement and hope. When I spoke of this paradox to him, he reminded me that he had often told me to look at things "upside down" or "from the other side of the coin" and that this very paradox, this "stick with two ends," while a potentially dangerous thing was also a very useful tool—in that it could give stimulus of such an order that one sometimes found energy and strength to work against odds that seemed impossible. He also said that any efforts of less than "super-human" strength were of no value anyway, once more pointing out that, in a sense, man's only hope was to fight to attain the "impossible." The only thing worth doing being something that "could not be done."

X

Perhaps because of the nature of his work and the problems of his students, Gurdjieff often discoursed on the question of good and evil. Basically, as he frequently pointed out, there are no such things as good and evil except as they exist in the form of moral concepts in the mind of man. But since his work dealt with mankind and since mankind, individually, was preoccupied with both good and evil they did, therefore, exist as problems in the sense that if one believes that something exists, it does exist—in this sense, mind is reality.

In an objective sense, Gurdjieff preferred what he called "objective morality"—a morality based on individual conscience and not on any social definitions of good and evil. In this sense, evil could be considered a term for whatever was improper to man as a function or a manifestation—anything that harmed an individual or his fellow men. In this limited sense, i.e., that good and evil exist if you think they do, Gurdjieff insisted that man's potentiality to manifest either good or evil was always equally strong and that it, in fact, grew as man learned more and developed more. While I had often heard arguments against this theory, it seemed simple and logical enough to me. As man learns and grows, his general potential, and his power, increases. It seems natural, therefore, that if one subscribes to moral concepts defined by the words "good" and "evil," man's potentiality to act in either sense is automatically increased. Surely Hitler and Stalin, together with millions of their followers, were convinced that their aims, and therefore their means of achieving them, were "good."

A good deal of misunderstanding entered into any discussions on this subject, largely because it is difficult for any large group of individuals to define what is good and what is evil, and then to agree on such definitions. It seems to me that when Gurdjieff used the terms he was using them in a special and rather narrow sense: referring to the constructive and destructive forces in man as related to his own growth and development. For example, he frequently warned that his work could only become more difficult as one learned more; in other words, as one grew one did not achieve any greater peace or any visible, or tangible reward—one did not become obviously "good"—but the struggle between any individual's capacity for "good" or "evil" for himself became that much more intensified. Mr. Gurdjieff himself, was an interesting example of this particular theory and I often thought that his personal power was such that he could very easily do as much harm as he could do good. When he advised a woman to give up her very well-paid position and incur debts in order to rid herself, finally, of her preoccupation with financial security, there were many people who thought this was "evil" advice, as there were those, also, who thought it "good." It depended, finally, upon the interpretation given to the advice by the woman in question and the effect it had on her. (Incidentally, she followed his advice, and had to struggle for years to get out of debt; she thought it was an experience that contributed to her growth and understanding of life and of people, as well as something that did free her from her unconscious involvement with security.)

Because of the effect of Gurdjieff—the impact of his presence—on people, it was necessary for him to exercise a great deal of judgment in his dealing with them, particularly since most people came to him with a preconceived idea of his abilities and his teachings. Such preconceptions were usually not founded on any truth or fact and were only likely to be increased once the person concerned had actually met him. Because of his reputation, people rarely met an individual named Gurdjieff—they met a picture of him that had previously formed in their minds. A person who was convinced that Gurdjieff was dealing in "evil" black magic, on meeting him, would interpret anything he might say or do as proof that he was a "black magician."

Many years ago, Aleister Crowley, who had made a name for himself in England as a "magician" and who boasted, among other things, of having suspended his pregnant wife by her thumbs in an effort to produce a monster-child, made an unsolicited visit to Gurdjieff in Fontainebleau. Crowley was apparently convinced that Gurdjieff was a "black magician" and the ostensible purpose of his visit was to challenge Gurdjieff to some sort of duel in magic. The visit turned out to be anti-climactical as Gurdjieff, although he would not deny his knowledge of certain powers that might be called "magic" refused to demonstrate any of them. In his turn, Mr. Crowley also refused to "reveal" any of his powers so, to the great disappointment of the onlookers, we did not witness any supernatural feats. Also, Mr. Crowley departed with the impression that Gurdjieff was either (a) a fake, or (b) an inferior black magician.

Gurdjieff did use the terms "good" and "evil" in a rather simple, direct sense when he said that it was evil for a man not to honour his parents; that a "good" man, of necessity, did honour them. I think, also, that he would have classified murder as "evil," but beyond such obvious examples he made no pronouncements one way or the other. Certainly, a great part of his teaching was an attempt to help his students rid themselves of the ordinary concepts (moral) of both good and evil, and to replace their ordinary morality with an objective morality based upon the needs and dictates of conscience and that which was proper and natural to individual men. He insisted, however, that it was necessary to live one's life fully—within the framework of society—and that in order to do this and not be conspicuous, one had to subscribe, in public at least, to the prevailing social morality—in other words, it was necessary to "act" out one's role on the stage of life, but always to be able to differentiate between the outer "acting" man and the inner "real" man. He said that it was extremely difficult for anyone to do this properly, since the differentiation was often difficult to make— most people "acted" out their lives under the impression that they were living, when they were in fact, only reacting to life as it happened to them. He stated that, contrary to the principles expressed in the "Sermon on the Mount," as it was frequently interpreted, it was necessary to "hide one's light" from the ignorant and the uninitiated as they would only, quite automatically, attempt to destroy any such "light" or "knowledge"; however, it was equally important not to hide that same knowledge or "light" from oneself and from others who were working seriously and honestly towards the same goals of self-development and proper growth.

XI

MR. GURDJIEFF RETURNED TO EUROPE in the late thirties and, while I did not know it at the time, I was not to see him again for many years. I had been seeing him regularly in New York while he had been there but I had not had much serious, personal contact with him. Before he left, however, I had a long talk with him during which he reiterated the fact that it was proper for me to go out and "experience" the world; that whether I was aware of it or not, I had "absorbed" enough material—at least for the time being—and that the important thing for me was to live life and put that material to use in whatever situations I might find myself. He did not, specifically, recommend that I disassociate myself from his work or from the American groups, but when I questioned him about that he said that it was a question that would determine itself—that it was entirely up to me to do whatever I felt I should do about it.

During the ensuing years I did participate from time to time in group meetings and attended occasional readings of his books, but not for any long, sustained periods. In spite of this, there was no question of the influence which he still had over me. Rather like a child who considers a parent *the* final authority, I found that I never made any important decisions without at least attempting to consider them from the point of view of his teaching and I found, somewhat to my own surprise, that I tended to judge myself and others from a strongly moral and rather "puritanical" point of view. I was still young and relatively inexperienced and my judgments were likely to be harsh and very stern. Whether this was a result of my association with Gurdjieff (who was more "puritanical" or "righteous" in many ways than one would imagine) or simply an outcropping of my puritanical, middle-western American background, I am not sure, but as time passed I began to feel that a great deal of it stemmed from an unconscious reaction against his authority and an equally unconscious attempt on my part to free myself from his powerful influence. In any case, it was a genuine struggle, complicated by my strong feelings about Gurdjieff as a man and, as it were, a parent, and my equally strong "disapproval" of the behaviour of a great many of his followers.

An example of the conflict in me was that while I rejected most of the followers and would not attend their meetings, I continued, almost without knowing it, to revere him personally. There could have been no better illustration of this than when I met P. D. Ouspensky, his one-time student, who was conducting lectures and meetings in New York. I was told that he had announced a special series of lectures for persons who had, at any time, been associated with Mr. Gurdjieff, and, much against my better judgment, I was persuaded to attend the preliminary lecture which was to be a sort of introduction to the series.

A large group of Gurdjieff followers met Ouspensky at an apartment in New York where we listened to an interminable reading—quite incomprehensible to me—after which Mr. Ouspensky announced that he would answer any questions that any one of us might have before we "enrolled" (or did not enrol) for the ensuing lecture series. Various questions were asked and answered, but the only question that was of any interest to me was: "Why had Ouspensky 'broken' with Gurdjieff and publicly disassociated himself from the Gurdjieff work?" (In order to clear up any possible confusion, I would like to point out that one rumour had it that Gurdjieff had "dismissed" Ouspensky; but at the beginning of this "preliminary lecture" Ouspensky had stated that, whatever we might have heard to the contrary, it was he who had left Gurdjieff. Gurdjieff, characteristically, had never said anything about the break, one way or the other.) Ouspensky smiled at the question and said that the answer was very simple: When he had found out that "Gurdjieff was wrong" he had had to leave him—adding that the details of this discovery would be covered in the lectures to follow. I replied, with much greater feeling than I would have expected of myself, that I did not need to hear any more. It was a revelation to me to find that I was so fiercely loyal to Gurdjieff and to find that I was so positive that he could not have been "wrong" about anything. I did not attend any of Ouspensky's future lectures and those who did were only able to tell me that they had been very interesting and that I should not have missed them.

Some years later there was a reconciliation between the Gurdjieff and Ouspensky "factions" and I believe that Ouspensky's books—especially *In Search of the Miraculous*—are recommended as reading for prospective Gurdjieff students. I have no personal information about this reconciliation as I was not present when it happened and have had no contact with any Gurdjieff—or other—group for about fifteen years. Ouspensky's books, especially *In Search of the Miraculous* and *The Fourth Way* are unquestionably almost required reading for anyone interested in Gurdjieff; but it is perhaps needless to add that Gurdjieff's own published and unpublished books—assuming that one has sufficient interest and stick-to-it-iveness to actually read them—are the only ones that give a real and undiluted flavour of the man and his teaching.

Although I had championed Gurdjieff in the face of Mr. Ouspensky, my subsequent reaction to my own outburst took me somewhat by surprise, although it only came over me very gradually: I was sick and tired of all would-be Messiahs, prophets, mystics—from Kahlil Gibran and William Blake (always associated in my mind because of their drawings) up to and including Ouspensky, Gurdjieff, Buddha, and Jesus Christ himself. It was a good, healthy, and angry reaction, and it was—at least momentarily—liberating. However wise, all-seeing, and powerful these individuals might be, it was finally necessary—or so it seemed to me—to judge them by the more obvious, and more hard-boiled truisms that they themselves sometimes quoted. "Birds of a feather...," "... the company they keep," etc., as well as what now seemed to me to be an increasingly honest viewpoint: their accomplishments in terms that were comprehensible to me. I was not unaware of the fact that it was possible, if not quite likely, that I simply was not equipped to judge them—in other words, I was not a proper student for *any* philosophy—but the judgment had to be made, *for me.* Since I was not making it for anyone else, it was not likely to have any far-reaching harmful, or beneficial, influence.

I did not attempt to make any judgments about the dead. The main targets were the "seers" I had known myself; Ouspensky (I had known him at the Prieuré as well as during that brief encounter in New York) and Gurdjieff. I found that I did not know enough about Ouspensky to arrive at any conclusions of importance. I found, and find, *Tertium Organum,* and *A New Model of the Universe* and other writings of his wordy, over-intellectual, and generally incomprehensible—which is to say personally uninteresting. All of which is no judgment about their possible value.

As to Gurdjieff, I found that I did not criticize him from the usual point of view. By that I simply mean that I was not at all disturbed about his lack of morals in the usual sense; it did not matter to me that he had illegitimate children, that he drank a great deal, or that he might have been a "magician" or a "charlatan" or, as he called himself—a "devil." But if, in the final analysis, growth depended upon individual effort, if it was all "up to you" anyway, then why be a Messiah? Who, besides Gurdjieff himself, thought or knew that he was *chosen* or that he was unable to be anything other than a teacher? As an individual man, I knew him well enough to have very great, genuine affection for him.

As a teacher…well, that was a completely different question. I could accept him in that role as I would accept the "teaching" which a parent gives to his child—it is a proper responsibility and an obvious one: the child is his. But as a leader of mankind? He must be, I concluded, just as fanatic and just as star-struck (although by something other than himself) as his pupils. Maybe. Maybe not. My "conclusions" did not get me anywhere, except to conclude that I did not have the proper "faith" or that I had not—in relation to Gurdjieff—"seen the light." But it was a relief to have wrestled with the problem. In a curious sense, I ended up liking him, as a person, even more. He began to seem to me in a very literal, paradoxical sense, the embodiment of that excellent phrase: "a real, genuine phony." That *he*, but not necessarily everyone else, grew in such a way that the evil and the good within him progressed equally—I accepted whole-heartedly. But not for myself. I was on the side of something—even if I didn't know what it was. I wanted to believe in "good," and I wanted to fight for it. I suppose it was something like suddenly finding out that you believe in God.

This "state of being" of mine did not last for very long. The simple fact of World War II put an end to most of my feelings, in fact to almost any "religious" feelings in me—but even so, it was near the end of the war that I had my most shattering and important contact with Gurdjieff.

XII

EVEN NOW, I FIND IT difficult to describe my next meeting with Mr. Gurdjieff, in the late summer of 1945, a few weeks before the first atom bomb fell on Japan. Any description of that meeting must necessarily be preceded by an account of, and an explanation for, my personal state at that time.

I had been employed from 1940 to 1942 in New York and Washington—working mostly for the British government—and had become very much involved, emotionally, with the "war effort." At the time of my draft call, there was some consideration of the possibility of my being deferred, but on the whole I felt that it would be somehow "wrong" for me to avoid the experience of actual war and I made no effort to obtain any deferment.

I was absorbed into army life rapidly enough, although I was completely appalled by it and by the people with whom I came into contact. I was certainly aware of the truth that one tends to lead one's life within a small social circle of one's own kind and class—I felt that I had never even known of the existence of many of the types and classes of people I met in the course of my first few weeks in the service.

Once overseas, and quite without any awareness of my own, I began to be unconsciously filled with horror at the effects of war. My American upbringing—in spite of several years in France as a child—had certainly been no preparation for mass bombings and other such horrors. However, as I have said, I was not aware of these reactions at all at the time. I had a good behind-the-lines secretarial job (or so I thought) and contented myself by simply doing a reasonably efficient piece of work as my part in the war. Since the army, day by day, is primarily boring, I was happy to be busy enough not to have time to do any active thinking. But any strong, even if buried, feelings must somehow and sometime find expression, and after several months I gradually slid into a long-term depression. Along with this depression I began to overeat and to gain weight. This was followed by something that was grimmer than any depression. I had a series of what seemed to me to be miraculous escapes that began to take on an air that was, to me, almost sinister. I will describe two of them, as examples: On one occasion, while on manœuvres in England, I was working at my desk in the "command" tent, in the company of several officers—nine or ten, at least. There was, as usual, an air raid going on at the time but no one was paying much attention to it. I got up and left the tent to go to the field latrine and during that short absence, a bomb hit the tent and everyone in it was blown to bits. To make it eerier, my typewriter landed within a few feet of me, in excellent condition.

Another time, while on a weekend pass at Torquay on the southern coast of England, I was standing, with another enlisted man, against a building overlooking the park below us. Without any air raid warning we were suddenly being strafed by six German fighter planes which had come in "below" the radar, almost at sea level. It had happened so quickly that neither my friend nor myself did anything at all...we simply stood there, dazed. A great many people in the park were killed and when one of the planes strafed the building where we were standing, my friend was cut in two by the bullets, which missed me by a few inches although we were not more than three feet apart.

As I have said these were only two of the incidents—and there were many more—that began to have a curiously sinister effect upon me. At first, my reaction was one of wonder—why was it that I was the one who had not been killed? And there was a period when I almost believed that I was leading a "charmed" life, that I had been in a sense selected, or chosen, not to be killed. But as time wore on and there were more and more such escapes I began to resent them actively. I watched so many of my fellow-men die during that period that I began to wish that I could die in their stead. The enormity of war—the very fact of it—was more than I could comprehend, and as it continued to proceed senselessly and endlessly, life itself seemed to me to lose whatever meaning it had had—and I was not at all sure that it had any. There were no feelings of righteousness, patriotism, or loyalty that could conceivably justify such wholesale murder and I had very grave doubts about the meaning of human existence. I thought of Gurdjieff frequently during those days, trying to imagine how he would explain, if he could, the act of war, but I was unable to imagine any answers or explanations that he might have had.

Finally, on the continent after D-day, the problem became of such importance to me that I could not think about anything else and I came very close to the edge of a complete nervous collapse. When I was faced with hospitalization, I somehow managed, in my highly nervous state, to convince my commanding officer, a general, to give me a pass to go to Paris where I would be able, I hoped, to see Mr. Gurdjieff. I don't know, even now, quite how I was able to convince the general. We were stationed in Luxembourg at the time and there was a standing order that no one from that area was to be given any liberty in Paris, except for the most important reasons. Also, I do not know what reasons were given in my case, but I had apparently made an impression on the general for he did obtain special permission for me.

When I left for Paris, I had not slept for several days, I had lost a great deal of weight, had no appetite and was in a state very close to what I would have to call a form of madness. Even now, while I can remember the long train trip vividly (all the railway lines had been bombed and we were shunted backwards and forwards over a large part of Belgium and France in order to reach Paris) I remember, especially, my conviction that unless I managed to see Gurdjieff I would not be able to go on living. After an interminable ride, and thanks to a sergeant in the carriage with me who managed to force coffee and brandy down me and keep me wrapped in blankets during the night, we finally reached Paris. In one way, Paris itself—which I had learned to love as a child—was a kind of tonic and gave me a spurt of energy, at least enough to help the sergeant find a hotel room and to start me on my search for Mr. Gurdjieff, as I had no idea where he lived. The telephone book and the "Bottin" were of no help to me and, in my peculiar psychological state, I began to despair. I managed, somehow, not to lose my head, and did eat a good dinner. After that, I set out methodically to try and remember the names of some of his students whom I had known in the past and who might be in Paris then.

I had arrived in Paris at about four o'clock in the afternoon and it was not until after nine that evening that I finally located an older woman who had been at the Prieuré when I had been there as a child. She not only assured me that Mr. Gurdjieff was in Paris and that I would certainly be able to see him the following day, but also offered me a room for the night. I accepted gratefully and talked with her until very late, which relieved my nervousness to some extent. Even so, I was still convinced that I had to see him before I could relax and I did not sleep very well that night.

I had to spend most of the morning—fidgety and anxious—in the company of my benefactress, as she assured me that I would not be able to locate him—I no longer remember why—until about noon. At eleven o'clock, she gave me two addresses: one of a café where he habitually had coffee in the late morning, and the other of his apartment. I went to the apartment first, but he was not there. I then went to the café and he was not there, either. I became very irrationally upset and began to think that I had lost my way in Paris (if not my mind), so I telephoned the lady, telling her where I was and that I had been unable to locate Mr. Gurdjieff. She did her best to reassure me and suggested that I go back to his apartment—I had not, she was able to assure me, lost my way—and wait for him there. I followed this suggestion and went back. I could not get in to the apartment, but the aged concierge, who seemed alarmed at my desperate appearance and manner, brought an armchair into the hall and placed it so that it faced the entrance, and told me to try and rest—that he was sure to arrive very shortly.

I waited for what seemed to me an interminable length of time, forcing myself to remain seated in the armchair, staring at the entrance. It was probably not more than about one hour later when I heard the sound of a cane tapping on the sidewalk. I stood up, rigid, and Gurdjieff—I had known it must be he, although I had never known him to use a cane—appeared in the doorway. He walked up to me without the faintest sign of recognition, and I simply stated my name. He stared at me again for a second, dropped his cane, and cried out in a loud voice, "My son!" The impact of our meeting was such that we threw our arms around each other, his hat fell from his head, and the concierge, who had been watching, screamed. I helped him retrieve his hat and cane, he put one arm around my shoulders and started to lead me up the stairs, saying: "Don't talk, you are sick."

When we reached his apartment, he led me down a long hall to a dark bedroom, indicated the bed, told me to lie down, and said: "This your room, for as long as you need it." I laid down on the bed and he left the room but did not close the door. I felt such enormous relief and such excitement at seeing him that I began to cry uncontrollably and then my head began to pound. I could not rest and got up and walked to the kitchen where I found him sitting at the table. He looked alarmed when he saw me, and asked me what was wrong. I said I needed some aspirin or something for my headache, but he shook his head, stood up and pointed to the other chair by the kitchen table. "No medicine," he said firmly. "I give you coffee. Drink as hot as you can." I sat at the table while he heated the coffee and then served it to me. He then walked across the small room to stand in front of the refrigerator and watch me. I could not take my eyes off him and realized that he looked incredibly weary—I have never seen anyone look so tired. I remember being slumped over the table, sipping at my coffee, when I began to feel a strange uprising of energy within myself—I stared at him, automatically straightened up, and it was as if a violent, electric blue light emanated from him and entered into me. As this happened, I could feel the tiredness drain out of me, but at the same moment his body slumped and his face turned grey as if it was being drained of life. I looked at him, amazed, and when he saw me sitting erect, smiling and full of energy, he said quickly: "You all right now—watch food on stove—I must go." There was something very urgent in his voice and I leaped to my feet to help him but he waved me away and limped slowly out of the room.

He was gone for perhaps fifteen minutes while I watched the food, feeling blank and amazed because I had never felt any better in my life. I was convinced then—and am now—that he knew how to transmit energy from himself to others; I was also convinced that it could only be done at great cost to himself.

It also became obvious within the next few minutes that he knew how to renew his own energy quickly, for I was equally amazed when he returned to the kitchen to see the change in him; he looked like a young man again, alert, smiling, sly, and full of good spirits. He said that this was a very fortunate meeting, and that while I had forced him to make an almost impossible effort, it had been—as I had witnessed—a very good thing for both of us. He then announced that we would have lunch together—alone—and that I would have to drink a "real man's share" of fine old Armagnac.

As we ate an enormous lunch, drinking glass after glass of Armagnac, he told me to talk, just to talk about whatever had been troubling me. I found it difficult to begin for at that moment I had no troubles at all. I felt wonderful. But once I had begun, I was able to describe my entire history since I had last seen him, summarizing easily and using a form of "shorthand" which seemed completely natural to us both. He listened without comment, then said finally that what I had told him was of no real importance—nothing to worry about—and asked me how long I would be able to stay in Paris. I told him I had three days and he said that I was to come to his apartment for lunch and for dinner every day during that time, but that the rest of the time I was to go out and "play." "One thing you never learn," he said quietly and affectionately, "is how to play, even though I try to teach you this when you child. Now, you go out and do *anything* that will amuse you, any kind of play, then come back here at ten o'clock." I asked him what was going on before ten o'clock and he said there was going to be a meeting. When I suggested that I should come to that, he said, laughing: "No, do not come to meeting with disciples. This not play and you already too serious." He said that I could, of course, have the room he had offered me but that if I could stay elsewhere it would be better for me as there were too many people coming and going at all hours in the apartment, and to see what I could arrange about some other place to stay.

I left him, made arrangements with my hostess of the previous evening to stay with her, and, following his advice, played for the rest of the day.

XIII

THE RETURN OF MY ENERGY was not a momentary thing. I was still feeling wonderful when I returned to Mr. Gurdjieff's apartment at ten o'clock that evening, and after introducing me to a large group of his students as his "*real* son," who had been at his "real school," he immediately put me to work in the kitchen. Once again, he seemed very tired, and he left me in charge of the food while he went off to "rest." For the second time that day he was gone for fifteen minutes and when he reappeared I was struck once more by his renewed strength and energy.

We had a very lively—and for me—very amusing supper. We still communicated with one another in a kind of "shorthand" which was both amusing and irritating to the other guests; irritating largely because, to his apparent delight, I found most of his conversation extremely funny and could not refrain from laughing which only served to increase his amusement. The other guests were confounded largely because his remarks did not seem, on the surface, funny to them. There was one woman present who seemed especially irritated with our laughter because she spent most of the time asking his advice about various serious problems. As he listened to her questions he would wink at me and—the first time—told me in Russian, that if I listened carefully I would learn how funny the "truth" could be. She said, among other things, that being rich she felt that she was at a disadvantage in her understanding of his work and that she often assumed that her so-called friends would not really like her if she did not have any money.

Gurdjieff said that the solution to these problems was simple enough: (1) She could give her money to him, knowing that he would make good use of it; (2) She could then live among the poor and would quickly learn—since she would have no money—whether or not she had real friends. As to "understanding" his work, he said that she would have to learn first, to understand. His replies were so obvious and so typical of him when people insisted upon questioning him at meals which were, always, a period of diversion for him, that I could not help laughing which, again, amused him a great deal. When she objected to our laughter, he said that she should learn, as I had recently learned, that laughter was, in *truth*, a very good medicine.

When we had finished our supper, he dismissed everyone but told me to stay and help him with the dishes. We did the dishes together and then retired to a small room—a sort of pantry with various foods and herbs hanging from the ceiling and stored on the shelves—where we drank coffee and he played on his harmonium. He played much of the music I had known at the Prieuré, and although we did not talk very much at first, it was a rather sentimental, emotional reunion. When he finished playing, he broke our mood suddenly by asking me if I didn't need some American cigarettes. Once more, I began to laugh, since cigarettes were not only plentiful at that time in the army, but also very cheap. He laughed with me and said that it was a great pleasure to enjoy laughter with someone again—that one of the saddest aspects of his life was that his students were so impressed with him that they could never condescend to anything so low as laughter. I told him that I agreed with this but that I felt, as I had told him once before, that it was his own fault—that he put "the stars in their eyes." He agreed readily, and seemed pleased that I would "kid" him, as he put it. I said then that while I had refused the cigarettes, I would like to give him something and offered him several thousand francs which I had "made" on the black market—by trading in various currencies; an art which I had only learned recently. He looked at the money for a moment and then asked, seriously: "Why you give me this?"

I said that it was a sum which I had "made out of the blue" and illegally, and that I thought he could have more fun with it than I could. He smiled at my reply and then said, thoughtfully, that he had thought that I had intended the money as "payment" for something. I said quickly that I thought that money could only pay for "things" and that this money because of its origins, the way I had acquired it, was really "play" money, and that while I had certainly needed to play—he did, also. He was satisfied with this and agreed to take it on that basis, but only if I would accept a carton of cigarettes. I laughed and said I would and he then said that it was important to exchange "useless presents" from time to time.

He then referred to his conversation with the woman at the supper table and said: "You see what trouble I have with students? She ask stupid questions and I give stupid answers, but even though stupid, they honest. But same is true even when someone—very rare—ask genuine question. When I give true answer, her unconscious already know answer is true because unless already know answer, unconscious cannot ask question. But, even so, she think I make joke, so will not listen. In teaching is necessary to remember that no one really asks questions. Impossible to ask question about something you not already know, already have good idea. So I only give answers which she already know. Answer to such question everybody already know. Is usual, when person ask me question, to already know two answers: one pleasant, one unpleasant. Not really ask question, only want confirmation; want pleasant answer from other person than self, because already know pleasant answer not right. But...*if* other person, like myself, give pleasant answer then can say to self that I tell this answer, and so not have to worry with conscience because is *my* fault. But for serious man is not necessary find new answers, but new questions. Once you ask question, this mean you already have very good idea about answer. For teacher is important make student ask new question. This reason why education in your country and in modern times is upside-down. Teacher in school never make new student ask new question or try to discover new thing. Only answer old questions to which everyone already have answer or can find answer in self without effort."

He poured coffee and Armagnac for us again and then went on: "This woman not take me seriously and so will not discover anything. What I tell her is truth. If she could give up money and have to live like poor person she would create possibility for two things. First, would find out what other people like, how they live, and also find out much about herself, that she stupid, shit-person, only have value of her money. Cannot be understanding between rich and poor, because rich and poor, both, only understand money. One understand life with money and despise people without money. Other understand life without money and hate people who have money. This woman now hate self because guilty about being rich. Poor man hate self—or sometimes just life—because feel guilty about not having money or feel cheated by world. With such unreal, false attitude, impossible understand any serious thing like my work. For instance, this woman tell that I most important influence in her life—but would be impossible for her to give me her money—so, very simple, she not tell truth. I not important for her life, but only her money important. With poor man can be same thing. Can believe in me and what I teach only if I first teach how to make money—this what poor man think. Not so. If I teach him how make money, then he will have only other problem—he will not be able to live without this money. But such people can learn important thing if can make effort in self to give up money—or, if poor, to give up desire for money. Impossible to do my work with all energy if also concerned with money. But all these things very difficult for your contemporaries. Not only cannot do. Cannot even understand why this question of money important. Such people will never understand real teaching or real possibility of learning anything."

He smiled at me, reminiscently, and then went on: "You remember Prieuré and how many times I have struggle with money. I not make money like others make money, and when I have too much money, I spend. But I never need money for self, and I not *make* or earn money, I *ask* for money and people always give, and for this I give opportunity study my teaching, but even when they give money still almost always impossible for them learn anything. Already, they think of reward... now I owe them something because they give me money. When think of reward in this way, impossible learn anything from me."

XIV

EXCEPT FOR THE FACT THAT there were no grounds and gardens in which Mr. Gurdjieff's students could labour, the "teaching" of his method did not seem to me to have changed very much. There were still readings, lectures, dance groups, and interviews with particular students. The only thing missing in the general ambience was "The Prieuré" itself. On the other hand, there was a change—at least it was new to me—in at least a part of Gurdjieff's own activity.

I noticed almost immediately that there were a number of daily visits at his apartment by older people, most of whom did not appear to have much, if anything, to do with his "work." Not only were they old, but they all appeared to be poor. Gurdjieff's attitude towards these people bore little resemblance to his treatment of those persons who were, quite obviously, his students. He treated them with courtesy, kindness and, I gathered, generosity. During the course of one of our own private sessions in the "coffee room" I spoke, somewhat hastily, about this "retinue" and the fact that he appeared to me to be helping, if not actually supporting, a great many people who did not seem to be in any way involved in his work. I do not remember my own exact words, but I remember that the implication was that he was helping in the perpetuation of persons who, unless I had misunderstood him in the past, were—to use his phrase—nothing more than "fertilizer" and without any particular "possibilities."

Gurdjieff was not amused; on the other hand, he was not angry. Patiently, although I detected a note of irritation in his voice, he explained that I was confusing an issue and that I had not understood him completely in the past. In the first place, fertilizer *per se* was not a *bad* thing to be if there was—in this life—no other possibility, and, more to the point, if the given individual was not striving for some other destiny. "Not only you not understand this about my work," he said, "you also not understand about what kind of person I am."

After more coffee had been poured, and he had looked at me reflectively, he said: "I play many roles in life...this part of my destiny. You think of me as teacher, but in reality, I also your father...father in many ways you not understand. I also 'teacher of dancing,' and have many businesses: you not know that I own company which make false eyelashes and also have very good business selling rugs. This way I make money for self and for family. Money I 'shear' from disciples is for work. But other money I make for my family. My family very big, as you see—because this kind old people who come every day to my house, are, also, family. They my family because have no other family.

"I give you good example why I *must* be family for such people. You not know, even though you hear about this, what life is like in Paris during war, while Germans here. For such people—people who come to see me every day now—was impossible even find any way to eat. But for me, not so. I not interested in who win war. Not have patriotism or big ideals about peace. Americans, with ideals, kill millions of Germans, Germans kill—with own ideals—English, French, Russian, Belgian...all have ideals, all have peaceful purpose, all kill. I have only one purpose: existence for self, for students, and for family, even this big family. So, I do what they cannot do, I make deal with Germans, with policemen, with all kinds idealistic people who make 'black market.' Result: I eat well and continue have tobacco, liquor, and what is necessary for me and for many others. While I do this—very difficult thing for most people—I also can help many people."

I persisted: "But *why* did you do it? Why for *them?*"

He smiled. "You stupid still. If can do for self and students, can also do for others who *cannot* do such thing." He paused and then added, smiling enigmatically now: "Ask self why old lady, with very little money, every day feed birds in park. These people—this family—my birds. But I honest: I say I do this *for* people, and also for self. This give me good feeling. Lady who feed birds in park not tell truth. She tell only do for birds, because love birds. She not tell what pleasure she get."

My question now seemed to me somewhat silly, and I apologized for having asked about the "old" people.

He shook his head. "Not necessary be sorry. Is not bad question you ask me. But one more thing about this question. You notice all such people who come here are already old. Without me not have possibility die properly. Except me, such people not have family, and for future can only look towards death. If I help such people die in right way, this can be very important and very good thing. Someday you understand this better, but you still young."

XV

ALTHOUGH I WAS WITH MR. Gurdjieff constantly during my three-day leave in Paris, he did not refer to my condition or "illness" at the time of my arrival. He kept me with him, alone, after the dinners and suppers at which there were always many guests, and when he did talk to me privately it was about the problems of his students, or about his difficulties with them. He told me that it would have been interesting for me to have been in Paris at the time that he had suggested to a number of his students that the war and its aftermath had provided a proper climate in which to learn the importance of living in the present. He said that, mostly because of our habits and preconceptions, it was very difficult for people to understand what was meant by "living in the present." Too many people would interpret this as an excuse for casting caution aside and would live "dangerously" without thought for the future. What he meant by "living now" was to expend all one's energy on living completely at the moment—experiencing life as fully as possible in the consciousness that this moment—this *now*—will never exist again. To many people this seemed to mean living fully in the sense of staying awake too long, drinking too much, or adopting an attitude of "eat, drink and be merry, for tomorrow we shall die," which was not what he intended.

It was true, he said, that in order to live completely in the moment it was necessary to be aware of the inevitability of one's own—possibly imminent—death. However, such awareness was not to be taken as an injunction to experience as much as possible or to overdo as much as possible while one was alive, but rather to be conscious of what one was doing and to try to occupy oneself "properly"—in such a way that one's experience would contribute to one's growth.

While he would not define "proper" activities clearly—one had to discover "proper" and "profitable" experience and activity for oneself—he did advise exercises that would help any individual to concentrate on conscious activity. Almost all such exercises were—in one way or another—a form of learning something more about oneself. For example, a common exercise was to make a daily programme of activity for oneself, and to be able to foresee and allow time for inevitable interruptions or distractions and, especially, to plan a proper amount of "work and play" for a given period of time. He said that there was often value in over-reaching—doing more than one "could"—but that one could not over-extend one's energies and capacities consciously until one had learned, through such an exercise, just how much available energy, how large a capacity, and how much available concentration one had that was "ready for use." He said that any man, in a sense, had limitless energy, but that such energy was not available to him if regular habits, acquired from infancy, did not permit its expenditure—habits of sleep, need for food, etc. Almost everyone was unconsciously trained not to use all his energy; given such training it was impossible, suddenly, to begin to use it. In performing an exercise such as "programming one's activities" it was possible to find out a great deal about *self*. Usually, an individual would try to do too much, but this was not always a bad result because sometimes one could do "too much" without bad results and could learn: (a) that the planning was not accurate, and (b) that they did have more energy than they had realized. In the beginning, however, the purpose of the exercise was to be accurate and to plan exactly—failing to do exactly what was planned, or doing too much, were both incorrect and either under-doing or over-doing was to be *punished.* I asked him what kind of punishment and he said that the punishment "should fit the crime" and that the very selection of a fitting punishment was, in itself, an exercise. It was important, particularly, not to over-punish oneself.

As to living in the present, or "living now," Gurdjieff said that if I could tell myself honestly that during a given period of time—whatever I happened to be doing—I at no time thought of anything other than what I was doing, I would at least have experienced the feeling of concentration and total involvement in the moment. He said that, for young people before they were contaminated, a sexual experience could be used as a good example of "living in the moment," being "totally involved," but he added that as one grew up in the ordinary way even sex ceased to be as compulsive and totally absorbing and no longer commanded all one's energies and attention. Also, he made it very clear that he was using the example of sex only to describe the approximation of total preoccupation in the moment. Sexually, the involvement was unconscious—in life, it was necessary to achieve a similar degree of concentration and absorption in the moment purposefully and consciously.

As I say, he did not speak of these things in relation to me, particularly or personally, at the time, but when I asked him if he thought I should do any of these exercises he merely smiled and said that when a man was in a vegetable garden he would eat vegetables for a number of reasons: because he was hungry, because he was greedy, or because he was attracted to the vegetables for some other reason. It depended on the man and his need or desire for vegetables; the vegetables, on the other hand, if eaten, would always nourish the eater—even to the point of making him ill if he did not know when to stop.

XVI

ON MY LAST DAY IN Paris, Mr. Gurdjieff did finally refer to my reasons for coming to see him and, more specifically, to my condition or "state" at the time I arrived. He said that our reunion had been a good and necessary thing for me and that he was glad that I had come to him. As to my "state" he said that, before discussing it in detail, he would have to know, for sure, that I would be able to come back to Paris fairly soon. While I had no way of knowing how difficult this might be, I assured him that I would return in about a month, vowing privately that I would get to Paris even if I had to get there without proper leave papers.

Thus assured, he said that my "state" or "condition" was, perhaps unfortunately, natural to me for a great many reasons, including the fact that I had been, as he had told me in the past, "poisoned for life" by him and by his teaching. He added, however, that although such states might be natural enough to me they would be considered unnatural by the general run of people and might also be considered as illnesses, although such states were actually a form of what he called "nervous over-exposure"—when I was very tired (and he said this was true of many people) my "skin" became, as it were, thin. I lost that protective coating or "shell" which all human beings acquire naturally in the course of the growing years. He said that it could be a very good thing to be able to "shed one's shell" or "protective coating" at will, but that it was necessary to learn when and how to do this and not to be at the mercy of having it happen under stress.

He gave me various "secret" exercises to do ("secret" in the sense that they were designed for me alone and could be harmful if revealed to, and used by, others), and two or three definite injunctions. One of them was that I was to drink, privately, a certain amount of hard liquor every day—depending upon my particular "state" of the moment, which I would have to learn to judge accurately, and he said that he had insisted on my drinking a great deal while in Paris in order that he would have the opportunity to observe me and determine my chemical reaction to hard liquor. The next injunction was that I was to take a certain medicine daily and was to report to him when I next saw him on my reactions to it, and he gave me several dozen pills. He stressed the fact that I was not to take any other medicine, under any circumstances, but that if I should be forced to take anything else I should discontinue his medicine at once.

He said that it was very unfortunate for me that I had to return to the army at just that moment—that if he were able to keep me with him for from three to six months he would be able to teach me how to control and use my nervous system and my "states" properly, but that since I could not stay with him I would have to learn to do this by myself, which, he warned, might take many years. He also warned me that the exercises he was giving me were not only secret but also dangerous and that, under normal circumstances, he would not permit anyone to do them without supervision. He then said that I must remember that when he used the word "dangerous" he meant that they could result in death, which would seem very attractive to me under certain circumstances when I would be "at the mercy" of a nervous "state." He made me write down the various exercises and "rules" he had given me and said that I should memorize them—"burn them into your brain"—as quickly as possible and then destroy the notes I had made.

The last specific warning he gave me was that my sense of well-being which I had had ever since seeing him in Paris would only last for about a week or ten days after which there would be a general let-down; therefore, it was important that I work very hard during that short period of time in order to consolidate the temporary gains I had made, also in an effort to "cushion" the let-down, which might be very severe.

After this last session with him, Mr. Gurdjieff told me that he was very sorry there was nothing more he could do at the moment but that I was not to forget my promise to return to Paris as soon as I could, and definitely within a month. "This promise of yours," he said, "very important. May be difference between hope and no hope for you."

XVII

BEFORE I LEFT PARIS, THERE was one last dinner, during which Gurdjieff indulged in one of his favourite pastimes: urging one of the people present to tell an "anecdote" about one of Gurdjieff's encounters with a would-be student. The man who told the story at dinner was a self-styled *raconteur*, and the story itself is a typical example of what many people thought of as Gurdjieff's devious, and infuriating, methods.

The story concerned an Englishwoman, wealthy and well known, who approached Mr. Gurdjieff when he was, according to his custom, sitting at the Café de la Paix in Paris, surrounded by a number of his followers. The English lady introduced herself and was invited by Gurdjieff to join him at his table. She stated her business in a forthright manner: She had been told that Gurdjieff knew "the secret of life" and she had come purposely to find him and to find out from him just what that secret was. As an inducement, she showed him a cheque for the sum of £1,000.00 payable to him and which she promised to give him when the secret had been revealed to her.

Gurdjieff showed his usual interest in the cheque and then agreed to demonstrate the secret of life for the lady. He got up from the table, walked up to a well-dressed "lady" who was generally to be seen walking the sidewalk in front of the Café de la Paix—it was her "beat" or station—and with a profound bow, asked her if she would do him the honour of permitting him to buy her a drink. The lady had seen him many times and did not seem to think of him as a potential client, but having nothing better to do at the moment, she accepted his invitation although she did seem a little suspicious of his numerous companions. He held her chair for her, and then sat down opposite her, asked her what she would like to drink and ordered it. Something expensive.

When she had received her drink, Gurdjieff again thanked her for honouring him with her presence and then said that he had seen her many times, knew her to be a woman of good sense and many accomplishments, for which reasons he had decided to explain something to her. He began by telling her that, in spite of her knowledge and her experience, he would wager that she could not possibly guess who he was and where he was from. The lady suggested that he was probably from some part of Russia, but Gurdjieff assured her that he was not and that what seemed to be his Russian accent was merely part of his disguise. Not only, he went on, was he not from Russia, he was not even from this planet—the planet Earth.

The lady did not make any comment on hearing this but merely looked at her drink, then at him, and then at the assembled group, and seemed to decide that she would put up with his conversation in return for the drink.

Gurdjieff continued by saying that he came from a planet which was unknown to her, unknown in fact to anyone on the planet Earth and that his planet was named "Karatas."

As the lady still made no comment, Gurdjieff launched into one of his long, wordy explanations, this time concerning the difficulties—for the inhabitants of the planet Karatas—involved in living on the planet Earth. One of the greatest difficulties for beings like himself was the question of food, as most food produced on the Earth was completely unsuitable for organisms from other planets. For this reason, he continued, it was necessary for him, at great expense and with great difficulty, to have special food flown from the planet Karatas daily.

The lady finished her drink and was about to leave, a look of complete boredom on her face, when Gurdjieff ordered her another drink and assured her that he would not keep her much longer and that she would be adequately compensated for her time. Reassured, she stayed on but still refused to comment on his obvious flight of fancy. She did scrutinize his companions closely, her expression plainly suggesting that she had inadvertently become involved with a group of "nuts."

Gurdjieff then asked her if she would like to see some of the food which he imported daily from Karatas, and she shrugged her shoulders. He then produced a paper bag from which he took a few cherries. He said that while this "food" resembled a plant that also grew on the planet Earth it was, in reality, quite different. The lady finished her second drink and continued to stare at him.

"Would you be so gracious and so kind," he went on, "as to do me the great honour of tasting this superb fruit and telling me how it seems to you? What it resembles?"

Without a word the woman took two cherries from Gurdjieff's hand, put them into her mouth and ate them slowly. She removed the pits and dropped them into a saucer on the table. With undisguised sarcasm, she then stared at him and said, slowly and distinctly: "It seems to me that they are cherries." She then held out her hand.

Gurdjieff quickly pressed a few banknotes into her hand, stood up, made another obeisance in her direction, escorted her back to the sidewalk, bade her farewell and thanked her again for having rendered him a great service. She took a long look at all of his companions, shrugged her shoulders and walked slowly away, pocketing the money he had given her.

Gurdjieff then turned to the English lady, smiled at her and said, simply: "What you have seen is the secret of life."

The Englishwoman gave him a look of disgust, called him a charlatan and left, upon which Gurdjieff roared with laughter and returned to his writing. Inconceivable as it may seem, the Englishwoman returned to the Café de la Paix later that day, gave him the cheque, thanked him for what he had done for her and later became an ardent follower of his "system."

The laughter was general following this story, but one person present asked, quite seriously, why it was that knowledge—Gurdjieff's kind of knowledge—had to be presented in such a curious, devious, secret fashion—why could it not be made generally available to everyone, thereby benefiting everyone and improving the world in every way.

Typically, Gurdjieff avoided any discussion of his "devious" methods, but made a pronouncement about knowledge.

"Like almost all people," he said, "you not understand nature of knowledge. Knowledge, like very fine French champagne, is rare. There exists only a certain amount—and is impossible produce more. If you give everyone in world one drop of champagne, nothing would be changed, no one would appreciate it. But for people who understand French champagne, when they drink, they appreciate; also they have money to buy this. But even if everyone had enough money for such drink, even so they would not buy. While what I say is true—that existing amount of knowledge is limited; receptivity for such knowledge is also limited." He refused to say anything further, and that person only remarked that he was as mystified as before.

XVIII

I DID GET TO PARIS WITHIN a month to see Mr. Gurdjieff again—but during that period I came to feel that he had somehow known beforehand exactly what was going to happen to me before I saw him again. The details are of no particular interest, but among the "highlights" of that period are the facts that the predicted let-down was severe, I was hospitalized (where, oddly enough, my treatment at first consisted in having to drink a good deal of Cognac daily) and was, of course, unable to take his medicine for more than about ten days. In any case, I was not troubled about the medicine because I had had absolutely no reaction to it. I did continue to do the exercises that Gurdjieff had prescribed for me and I did, certainly, go through a "dangerous" period—a kind of self- and world-evaluation that seemed to shake my foundations—and during that period the predicted "death-wish" was very strong indeed. One saving grace during that month was that, sceptically, I wondered just how suggestible I had been when I was with Gurdjieff in Paris. Was I, as it were, unconsciously producing the climaxes that he had predicted might happen? The question, even though unanswerable, did serve to help me maintain some sort of balance and objectivity, and I was not especially concerned with finding an answer to it.

When I arrived in Paris again, I telephoned Mr. Gurdjieff and he made an appointment to meet me at a café later that morning. After we had met and while we were drinking coffee, we were approached by an elderly woman who proceeded to have a long conversation with Mr. Gurdjieff in Russian. I understood enough of their conversation to gather that it was primarily concerned with problems of health, finance, and the difficulty of obtaining sufficient food in Paris at that time. The black market, I knew, was flourishing, and while food was available, it was tremendously expensive.

At the conclusion of the conversation, the woman opened a package, wrapped in newspaper, and held up a small oil painting for us to look at. Mr. Gurdjieff asked her various questions about it: when she had painted it, and so forth, and finally bought it from her for several thousand francs. She thanked him effusively and I gathered that, thanks to his purchase, she would be able to afford to eat for a few more days.

When she left us, Gurdjieff sighed, handed the painting to me, asking me to carry it back to his apartment and hang it in the hall which was already lined with similar paintings—from the baseboard to the ceiling. When I had hung the picture, he asked me if I remembered Jane Heap ("Miss Keep," as he called her). I said that I did, of course, and he said: "You know, Miss Keep not have sympathy for my paintings. Last time she come here, I ask her what she think of my paintings, and she tell me: 'Mr. Gurdjieff, you have everything here, except art.' Miss Keep not appreciate what I do."

I could not help being amused by Jane's remark, but was interested in what he was going to say about it. He promptly went into a long harangue about art and the creative impulse, pointing out that it was particularly difficult for an artist to make money during the war, and that it was equally difficult now that the war was just about over. He went on to say that he did not collect art for his love of it, nor did he do it only from generosity and a desire to help the unfortunate artists. He said that it was very important...for that old lady...that someone should buy her art...because, in spite of what Miss Keep, or I, or anyone else, might feel about the quality of her painting, she had painted her pictures with her being—her real heart—and that it was very bad for any such creativity not to find an outlet; that is to say, a public, a buyer.

"I also get benefit from her art," he continued. "For in my house many people see her paintings and paintings of such other unfortunate people and they tell I have worst collection of paintings in Paris—perhaps in all world. I already unique to most people who know me, but in my collection of bad art people see that I am still more unique...in another way, unique."

After this "joke," he said, more seriously, "But, in truth, people could learn from this old lady. Unlike many people who know I generous and will help others, she never ask for money, but always only wish money for painting. She already understand what some 'intellectual' people not understand. If receive money, should give something for it."

After this lecture we prepared lunch and our first drink was, contrary to custom, a toast to the health and prosperity of the little old lady artist.

XIX

THIS VISIT TO SEE GURDJIEFF, made from the hospital with the assistance of an understanding military doctor, was very much like the previous one except that Gurdjieff dwelt on my condition at more length than he had before. He said that my non-reaction to the medicine he had given me only proved one thing to him—that I had an enormous, natural resistance to drugs, and should, therefore, avoid taking them whenever possible. As to drinking, he recommended that I continue to drink, but "consciously"—in the sense that I should learn to gauge accurately the needs of my system for alcohol. He insisted that I had such a need, but that it was periodic, and predicted that if I gauged the need properly I would go through periods where I would drink—or would need to drink—a good deal, and also sometimes through long periods when I would not need to drink at all; in fact, at such times, I would find that liquor might even be harmful for me. "As you grow," he added, "must remember that body can, without your awareness, make many changes in chemistry; may come time when you should never drink at all. Must try to live in tune with physical self and be conscious of all changes in own chemistry."

When he spoke of the various exercises he had given me, he made me tell him in detail how often I had done each one and also describe my reactions to each of them. He then told me to discontinue all of them and gave me two new exercises, again secret ones. When I began to make notes, he told me to tear up the paper and to stop writing. "These exercises you must learn in your heart, for ever," he said, "for in future there will be a time when you will need them and you will have nothing—not even a piece of paper. So must now memorize these exercises as the most important thing in your life. I tell truth when I say this—will be time in future when without such exercises you will die. Even with exercises will be very difficult for you to live."

I did not need any further admonitions, but in any case, he made me repeat these complicated exercises to him in complete detail several times before I returned to my unit. (I was not returning to the hospital; I had been discharged but given an extra three or four days to get back to my regular unit via Paris.)

The day I was to leave, Mr. Gurdjieff said that I would probably never see him again. "As you can see with own eyes," he said, "I now very tired and I know that when I finish this last book my work will be done. So now I can die, because my task in life is coming to an end." He looked at me gravely and continued: "This also mean that I can do nothing more for you ever. I know that now, in your heart, you already think about possibility of staying with me here in Paris after you get out of army, but you must forget this. I cannot help you any more, and besides you belong in your own country—America. So when you get out of army do not come back here but go home where you belong and where you will find much work for self, and many experiences."

Somehow, it was not a moment for emotion. He was very serious, very impersonal, and spoke without any visible feelings—it was almost as if he had been thinking aloud. He spoke of his death with such detachment and so convincingly that it was as if he was speaking of someone else. So, with no feelings or demonstrations, he finished talking and we went in to the usual enormous lunch, with many guests. As we ate, he told a great many stories and once again, he and I laughed a great deal. He urged one of his students to tell me the story of a visit with him to the American Embassy in Paris because of some complica-

tions over the question of obtaining a visa for Mr. Gurdjieff. It seemed
that a group of students had gone with him to the Embassy, armed with
various documents with which they hoped to prove that he had urgent
reasons for going to the United States. They were all told to wait when
they had arrived, and after a very short waiting period, Mr. Gurdjieff
got up and walked around the office distributing boiled sweets (from a
bag he carried in his pocket) to all of the stenographers and clerks. This
"sweet-giving" resulted in considerable pandemonium in the office,
and, of course, the official who was to review his application appeared
in the middle of it. Even so, the visa was obtained, but only after several
interviews and at great cost to the nervous systems of those who had
accompanied Gurdjieff.

Mr. Gurdjieff roared with laughter at this story and said it proved
conclusively that the world was mad. All he had done was generously
to offer sweets to some charming American girls and it had almost cost
him his visa.

At the end of lunch, Gurdjieff's mood changed very suddenly, and
when he rose from the table, I was worried about him. In the course of
a few minutes he had begun to look very ill. In spite of this, one of the
women at the table, one of the workers, leaped to her feet and rushed
to his side to ask him some question about whatever work—probably
translation—she was doing on one of his books. He supported himself
by leaning on a chair, and answered her questions slowly and concisely.
But, as he spoke, there was a definite change in the atmosphere in the
room. All of us—and there must have been about twenty persons present—rose from our chairs with one accord and waited silently. We were
all expecting something—I knew I was, and the tense faces of the others
indicated that we were one in this expectancy. When he had finished
speaking to the woman, he raised one arm and made a sweeping gesture
around the room, as if to command the attention of each one of us.

"Must make announcement," he said, dramatically, and in English.
(Several nationalities were represented, but all the people there, I knew,

spoke or understood English.) "My last book is now finished, except for work with editor." He paused, looked around the room, as if to examine each person, separately and intently, and then continued: "This mean my work is through—finished. This also have very important meaning for me. Mean at last I can die..." there was another pause, but his inflexion indicated that the sentence was not finished, "...but not just because book is finished. In life is only necessary for man to find one person to whom can give accumulation of learning in life. When find such receptacle, then is possible die." He smiled, benevolently, and went on: "So now two good things happen for me. I finish work and I also find one person to whom can give results my life's work." He raised his arm again, started to move it, this time with a finger extended and pointing, around the room, and then stopped when his finger was pointing directly at me.

There was an enormous silence in the room and Gurdjieff and I looked at each other fixedly, but, even so, I was aware that one or two of the others had turned to look in my direction. The tension in the atmosphere did not lessen until Gurdjieff dropped his arm, turned, and left the room. The rest of us seemed momentarily transfixed and I finally broke the seeming trance and walked across the room. I was stopped, abruptly, near the door, by a hand on my arm. It was a woman, one of the "instructors." She held my arm tightly in her hand, looked at me with a malevolent, sneering smile on her face, and said: "You will never learn, will you?"

I pulled my arm away from her hand gently. "What does that mean?"

She laughed. "How does it feel to be chosen?" she demanded. "From the look on your face, I can tell you exactly what you are feeling. He pointed at you, didn't he? And now—with your colossal ego—you march out of the room...the triumphant successor." I have to admit that I was feeling fine. I smiled back into her face, admitting to myself a feeling of genuine triumph, and said: "Your guess is as good as mine." Then I left the apartment.

I left Paris that afternoon, and returned to my army station.

XX

BACK IN THE ARMY AGAIN, I thought a great deal about my two visits with Mr. Gurdjieff in Paris, but it must have been two or three days after my dramatic departure from his apartment before I even attempted to evaluate my relationship with him or the meaning of that whole finale. When I began to re-live the "farewell" in my mind, I was forced to admit to myself that I had, at least momentarily, felt chosen. That, in fact, I still did. I was pleased with my behaviour at that moment—I had learned enough from him to be cagey about it when I had been accused by the lady—but the feeling of triumph was not unadulterated, and I was besieged by questions and doubts. I even went so far as to make a list of my doubts as I tried to think back over my entire experience with this man. The list began, more or less, as follows:

1. It is at least possible that he was actually referring to me as his "successor." It was possible on many counts:
   a. It was actually true;
   b. It was intended to "expose" my ego to myself;
   c. It was intended to produce various reactions in the other persons present;
   d. It was a huge joke on the devout followers.
2. What about my qualifications for the post?

    a. In all honesty, I was forced to acknowledge that as far as I was aware, I did not honestly know in what his "work" consisted. How then, could I carry it on?

    b. In what way, if any, was I different from the other members of his groups? Obviously, only in that I had always felt like a "lone wolf" and had never been able to participate whole-heartedly in the readings or other group activities.

3. Did I want to, assuming that I could, "carry on" his work—whatever it was?

    a. Yes, up to a point. Groups, dances, readings, no. But if there was some way in which I could "cull," as it were, what had seemed valuable in him to me from what had seemed, if not valueless, at least "incomprehensible," I would like to be able to pass it on in some way.

There were more questions—in fact they went on and on—and there were some tentative answers. My final answer did spring, some years later, from the ones I have listed above; at the time however, I was only confused and rather grimly determined to put the questions out of my mind. I realized that I had been moved, confused and perplexed by that last meeting, and my determination resulted in the decision that I would, somehow, manage to get to Paris once more before returning to the United States.

The war in Europe was over, and shortly after that last visit to Paris, the two atomic bombs were dropped on Japan, to the horror of most of us in the European Theatre. Like all other soldiers, I spent most of my time trying to hasten my own departure and speed up my return to America—not too easy because while I had a large number of "points"—more than I needed to get back—I was not married, and I was an officer by that time, having received a field commission. Married men and enlisted personnel had priority. I did, however, manage to get myself on the shipment list after some conniving and also wrote my own travel orders, routing myself through Paris on some sort of non-existent "official" business—a rather common practice in those days, as a "last fling" in Paris was practically obligatory, even though reasonably difficult to achieve.

As a result of all this, I did see Mr. Gurdjieff again, but it was completely unlike my previous visits. I found him, alone, at his apartment. He opened the door for me himself and was wearing a nightshirt, looking very sleepy. He gave me what I can describe only as a "cold" look and asked me what I was doing there. "Already I tell you goodbye, and already I think you in America. Why you come?" I was very "hurt" and said that I was on my way to America and that I had only come to say goodbye. He looked at me then, at least without hostility, and said: "Cannot say goodbye again—this already done." Then he gave my hand an impersonal, final shake. I did not say anything more, and since he had not asked me to come in, I turned to leave. He stopped me with a gesture, and then said sharply, and with a smile on his face: "Americans drop bomb on Japan, yes?" I nodded, and he went on: "What you think of your America now?" I was going to attempt to reply, but he closed the door gently in my face.

There had been, obviously, no time for questions. And, as I faced the door, I knew there never would be. If I have ever known anything in advance, positively, in my life, I knew something then: I would never see him again. And I didn't.

At that very moment, as I walked away from his apartment, I saw one huge question looming up before me: "What did you get out of your association with Gurdjieff? How has he affected your life? What did you learn from him?" I phrased it as three questions, but it is really one. I put it aside, then, deliberately. For the moment, at least, it was totally unanswerable. It remained unanswerable for many years. Until it, inevitably, reasserted itself.

XXI

WHEN I RETURNED TO AMERICA, I did become associated with some members of the New York group. Also, as he had predicted, I had a good deal of living to do and a great deal to experience on my own. But my questions, even though I did not allow them to come to the surface of my mind, were there, waiting to be answered.

The first time that I became strongly aware that they were still there was at the time of his death. My involvement with the Gurdjieff group in New York had come to a rather sudden end, and, as always, it was the attitude of his "disciples" which seemed to me the cause of my estrangement from anything having to do with his "work." In any event, someone did manage to track me down and tell me of his death and invited me to participate in a memorial funeral service which was being held in his honour in New York. I had a few doubts about my decision, but it was immediate. I did not go; it seemed to me at best an empty "honour" and he had died, as far as I was concerned, when I had last seen him in Paris.

After that momentary, and brief, re-awakening of my questions, I was able to put them away again—put them away, that is, in the sense of attempting to actually find answers to them. I could not put away all my thinking about Gurdjieff; in fact, I thought about him frequently and with considerable affection. I began to realize that at least a part of my mind was back in that old, well-established routine of reverence for him. I was, in reality, more reverent than I had ever been before. My reverence expressed itself in a kind of non-expression. I would not mention his name and would not identify myself with his work, except on the rare occasion when I saw people who knew of my association with him. But, inevitably, a part of my divided mind was, at least unconsciously, trying to answer my questions, or some part of them. There had been one major change in my thinking, however, that had come to me "out of the blue" and with that extraordinary flash of truth that frequently accompanies sudden bursts of insight. I knew that I was not, even remotely, any kind of "successor." But even this sudden knowledge, once the immediate convincing moment had passed, began to trouble me. Was I, perhaps, the successor after all, and simply refusing to admit it? The only partial answer I could find was that, even in death, he continued to have an enormous and troubling influence over me. I had learned enough from him about deviousness (not in any particularly derogatory sense), cleverness, and slyness to find myself wriggling through and around my own doubts and questions. Gradually however, I began to make a serious attempt to think about him other than in a personal sense—to dilute, as it were, the force of his still-powerful magnetism. I began to look at him differently. But the "light" was still too strong to do other than look at the fringes of the man and his work. I would try to take a quick glance at the man and the Prieuré—the nerve- and heart-centre of his activity—but in that picture, he was still too strong, too all-pervading. I decided to work from the outside in. How would I, how could I, talk about him and his work to a total stranger, for example? That proved easier, and my "explanation," such as it was, and as I began to try to analyse it, ran along these lines:

In addition to the Institute, in Fontainebleau, there were so-called "Gurdjieff groups" in London, New York, and Chicago, and perhaps elsewhere. The existence of these "groups" was, apparently, part of a plan to disseminate his teaching—eventually—throughout the world.

There were even small gatherings, which could not really be called "groups" since they usually did not have permanent leaders, in such culturally and physically remote areas as New Mexico. In the absence of established groups with leaders who had, at least ostensibly, the approval of Gurdjieff himself, the meetings were confined largely to fairly regular readings of his books which were available, before publication, in mimeographed form. In the United States, in these outlying areas, the people involved usually had permission from someone (such as a group leader in New York) to read the manuscript of *All and Everything.* The reading was the whole thing—no questions, no comments, no exercises, no dances, etc.

The New York and London groups were more highly organized, as was, for a time, the Chicago group. In addition to readings, there were dance or gymnastic groups and even lectures or interpretations of his teaching by the "leader." The one thing—the only thing—that all of these subsidiary groups had in common was the lack of Mr. Gurdjieff's presence, and it was an important lack. The readings, given the style of his writing, had value of a kind for the simple reason that the average person, no matter how interested he or she might be in the subject, would rarely actually finish his book if they were forced to read it alone. Generally speaking, the book is practically incomprehensible on first reading. It is somehow easier to be puzzled in a group, and in most cases it was only under these circumstances that the whole book would be read. The instructions in the beginning of the book are that it is to be read three times, and some of these smaller groups have managed to achieve such a record. The book has an impact that comes only with familiarity; in fact, it begins to have something of the power that is in the man himself. But beyond the further reading, then, of his subsequent books, I do not know what future there is for the readers.

At the time I was associated with them, the larger groups, at least, subsisted not only on readings, etc., but also on the ever-present possibility that they might someday actually see Gurdjieff in person—either they would manage to get to France to see him or, especially in the case of New York, he might make a visit to see them. While a great many of these groups had faithful and even ardent followers, none of them ever seemed to be more than carbon copies of the real thing. Even so, there was an infectious quality about the man that was often communicated even through his writing. If, after a certain length of exposure, his ideas and he, himself, were not rejected, they were accepted in a very special way. He became, to his followers, a genuine prophet—some sort of Messiah, if not some sort of God. It was apparently impossible to be simply interested. In the long run, it was almost automatic to be convinced or to lose interest—I suppose this is nothing more than a magnification of ordinary religious feeling. In any event, it would be terribly boring to attend Gurdjieff meetings *without* real conviction.

What then was Gurdjieff's purpose, and how was he trying to accomplish his aims?

Before either of these questions can be discussed—let alone answered—it is probably necessary to underline the fact that he had no purpose comprehensible to the average, relatively satisfied human being. A prerequisite to any understanding of his aims and an even relative acceptance of his means was dissatisfaction with the *status quo* in a personal sense, and dissatisfaction with, or distrust of, the state of civilization as we know it. His avowed aim, as stated in his book *All and Everything* is to "destroy" all contemporary habits, opinions, preconceptions, etc., concerning human existence; such destruction being a necessary condition for the reception and acquisition of totally new concepts about the potentialities of human existence.

In one of the few "political" statements he ever made in my presence he said that unless the "wisdom" of the East and the "energy" of the West could be harnessed and used harmoniously, the world would be destroyed. There could be a good deal of truth in that statement; in any case, given political events of our time, it does not seem particularly radical or unbelievable. It is, however, perhaps less easy to believe that Gurdjieff, alone, had the key to a system or a teaching that could accomplish the harnessing of east and west. The keystone of his teaching, of course, was that no progress—no human progress, that is—can be accomplished except on an individual level. Group work is valuable only in the sense that it helps the individual to achieve individual self-perfection. The group, as a whole, does not necessarily achieve anything at all, as a group.

He compared present-day human existence to a kind of larval stage in organic development; claiming that, as individuals, we have no concept of the potential capacities of human development and that every habit, custom, tradition, and tenet by which civilized man lives is, bluntly, not only unproductive but even evil or, at the least, negative. He dismissed all existing religions, philosophies and other systems of thought—*as practised*—as being worthless.

In view of this blanket criticism of human existence as we know it, he did not have a tremendous number of followers. But, it should be remembered, he did not want large numbers. He compared, in all seriousness, human life to any and all other organic life, plant or animal. Nature being profligate, there was, in his view, no reason to assume that a very large percentage of human individuals had any right to expect any other destiny than organic fertilizer for the general good of the planet. He did concede that humanity, unlike plants and other animals, had the possibility of achieving higher development; of, as he put it, "acquiring" a fourth body—or for the sake of convenience in terms, a soul. But he did not—even to his own followers—hold out this promise for everyone. In the same sense that each seed of every flower has the latent potentiality of producing a blossom, just in this sense does every human embryo have the potentiality of "producing" or "acquiring" a soul. In this connection, it is necessary to have in mind the number of seeds that do not even germinate.

These views are not, obviously, very flattering to the human ego, collective or individual. Even so, given my association with him, I do not find them particularly difficult to accept. There is an obvious logic in the cycles of nature in all other forms of life: why should man be excluded or in some way different? A flower, in its own way, may be aware of the possibility that it has the potentiality of blooming, and perhaps the seed that does not germinate suffers unimagined agonies somewhere in the process. Most individual human beings who had any relationship with—or exposure to—Gurdjieff's theories and ideas either rejected them completely or, I suppose, assumed that they, individually, had—through exposure to him—at least the possibility of "blooming"; i.e., of developing further into what he might well have called a proper human state.

In order to have anything to do with such a system of ideas, it is obviously necessary to believe in these basic concepts, and somewhere along the line to accept the view that we have only two choices: the rather general fate of being "fodder" or "fertilizer," or, the very slim chance of maturity. I say "slim chance" advisedly because, nature being nature, only a very small percentage of the whole—no matter how much they might desire it—had even the remotest possibility of growth.

If this view or estimate of the human condition has been accepted, it was then necessary—a sort of process of elimination was built in here—to accept that Gurdjieff, alone, had the method, knew the way to further development, or progress. If you have gone this far with him it becomes difficult to contend that he did not have the key. In other words, it became (or becomes) essential to believe in him in a total sense. The insidious, or compelling, aspect is that once exposed to his point of view it is almost impossible to refute or oppose it effectively. Who can say, positively, that his view of Nature and of man's place in Nature is wrong? If one looks at Nature objectively, if one studies animals, plants, birds, evolution—and finds natural logic in the various processes of growth—then on what basis does one except man in the sense that man is, automatically or inherently, divine or, to use a simpler word, different? Gurdjieff did not deny man's potential *divin-*

ity (although he did not use that word), he merely stated that it had to be acquired through conscious effort and what he called "intentional suffering," a process that is almost immediately regarded with suspicion by most people. The word suffering, particularly for the western world, seems to be a word that automatically denotes something that is to be avoided. Suffering, especially "intentional suffering," according to Gurdjieff, was not only not to be avoided, but as the expression implies, to be sought.

One of the most compelling arguments on his behalf was an unstated one. He was, obviously, not out to save the world; he did not care whether everyone was interested in what he had to offer. In fact, he said frequently that only a few people could be—underlining the fact that only a very few people could ever develop anyway. It is a great temptation to include oneself among the few.

Since my stay at the Gurdjieff school was for about four years beginning at a time when I was eleven years old, I do not think I can be considered as a convinced student. I have no idea whether Gurdjieff considered me or my brother or any of the other children, most of whom were there by the accidents of their birth, as students at all. We participated, as far as our capabilities would permit, in the daily work of the school but were not students in any other sense. We did not attend readings or listen to lectures on any regular basis—there was simply no rule about it and no one objected if we happened to be present. But even at my age I had a fairly good idea of how Gurdjieff induced "conscious effort" and "intentional suffering" in his pupils—or perhaps I should say how they were exposed to it. For the average person, it consisted largely in a preliminary period of joining in reasonably hard manual labour in a group. It could be anything from building a house to working in a garden and, at the beginning, it was simply hard work that was supposed to be done conscientiously. After a while, one became conscious of being thrust into somewhat frustrating circumstances having to do with the work—such as being forced to work with someone whose temperament clashed with yours; being taken off a job as soon as you became too interested in it, etc. Most of the novice students seemed to be put through a period of purposeful frustration. Inevitably, given the reputation of the school and its stated aims, they began to wonder just exactly what was being accomplished by doing physical labour, and nothing else. The frustration would usually increase because no one, including Gurdjieff, would answer their questions—they were simply told that for the time being they were to do as they were told. When they reached some kind of breaking point, they would suddenly be given an exercise—usually being told that they should observe themselves consciously while they worked and learn more about themselves. If they stayed long enough they were gradually taken into the inner circle where they attended readings or listened to lectures and participated in the exercises or gymnastics or dances, which purported to give them the opportunity to practise physical, mental, and emotional co-ordination simultaneously. After that...frankly, I don't know. Most of the people who stayed that long then began to have private interviews with Gurdjieff from time to time and I do not know what took place at such interviews. I do know that by that time, such people were generally convinced followers. They were convinced by the unquestionably extraordinary magnetism and perception of the man himself. As Katherine Mansfield once pointed out (see quote, page 114), "... he always acts at precisely the moment one needs it. That is what is so strange..."

There is no question but that this was so. There is no question that Gurdjieff had an unbelievable (unless you've seen it) *awareness* of other people. It was nothing so limited as mind-reading or thought transference. He seemed to know so much about the human processes, about the underlying logic in man, that he was conscious of everything that took place within any human being he happened to observe. It is the same kind of faculty that an occasional highly trained psychiatrist seems to have to a limited degree. Gurdjieff had it to an enormous degree, and I have never known him to be wrong—in my own case or in the case of any other people I knew. It was difficult to resist such obvious learning or "power" and, in fact, there was no reason to resist it. Contrary to the reports about him, there was no evidence that he did anything to anyone that could be considered "evil." The reported "evil" only came about through outward opposition. And a great many of his students brought it on themselves. There is nothing I know of better calculated to produce "opposition" and criticism on a rather vehement level than an attitude of almost beatific secrecy. His students, with contented, superior smiles on their faces would declare publicly that they had at last found the "real thing," or a "great teaching," etc., etc., and then, upon being challenged, seemed unable to explain what it was, or how it worked. I do not think it is "inexplicable," but I think the "method" or the "teaching" or what appears to be the "value" of his work simply cannot be communicated to people who have not had some experience with it themselves. It is primarily a question of values; the people who praise him unqualifiedly make the mistake of forgetting that they did not do so until they had experienced the impact of the man through working with him for some considerable length of time. The emotional experience that most people had with Gurdjieff and his work is not something that can be explained in a logical, convincing manner. He was idolized, believed in and adored—or hated and discredited. None of these attitudes can be considered as valid, nor do they explain him. I think it is probably fair to say that he was a genuine "mystic." And what does that mean unless mysticism is of some importance?

As to the critics and denunciators of Gurdjieff—and they are too numerous to name in anything except a long bibliography—most of them fell into one or two categories: they considered themselves students, and therefore critics, of any teaching that touched on the occult; or, they were disillusioned students of Gurdjieff's method. Those in the first category seem to me to pounce on him because he

did not live up to their conception of orthodoxy; as for the disillusioned and "vituperative" ex-students: If I found that Christianity,
for example, had failed for me, I would find it hard to blame it on the
Pope or the Bible.

XXII

I BEGAN TO FEEL THAT I was getting somewhere in my own thinking. I had even been able to touch on my personal experience at the Prieuré with some degree of detachment. I was pushed further along in my own questions by the judgments of a few other people. There are a number of "well-informed" and "sophisticated" people (Gurdjieff would have called them, derisively, the "intelligentsia") who know something about Gurdjieff and almost all of them know, for instance, that Katherine Mansfield, A. R. Orage, and P. D. Ouspensky were associated with him at one time or another. Many of these people will say, when Gurdjieff's name is mentioned: "Oh, yes, he's the man who killed Katherine Mansfield!" That is a direct quote, and, oddly, the judgment is nearly always phrased in those exact words. Because of this rather common catch-phrase judgment of him, it seems a good place for another look at him. Let me say, first of all, that I feel no great defensive urge to clear Mr. Gurdjieff of this accusation (which is perhaps less an accusation than a handy and rather dramatic means of identifying him); in any case, I have no direct information about the Gurdjieff-Mansfield relationship. She died at the Prieuré before I was ever there, and had she died in the arms or in the custody of some other individual or group, perhaps the accusation would be directed in that direction. Also, I do not think that Gurdjieff ever *killed* anyone.

I bring up the subject of Katherine Mansfield mostly because there has been a good deal of notoriety concerning their association. The surest and quickest approach to the Mansfield-Gurdjieff relationship must, it seems to me, be through Miss Mansfield's own words. Unfortunately, perhaps, Mr. Gurdjieff left no reports on the subject.

So, to quote Miss Mansfield:[1]

"I am going to Fontainebleau next week to see Gurdjieff. I will tell you about it. Why am I going? From all I hear he is the only man who understands there is no division between body and spirit, who believes how they are related. You remember how I have always said doctors only treat *half*. And you have replied: 'It's up to you to do the rest.' It is. That's true. But first I must learn how. I believe Gurdjieff can teach me. What other people say doesn't matter—other people matter not at all." (p. 671)

The only comment I can make on this particular letter is the rather obvious one that in the last sentence, the reference to other people seems to me to indicate an awareness of the fact that her decision will be criticized, that she knows that Gurdjieff is "suspect" to "other people" or perhaps only to John Middleton Murry. In any case, there is little question but that Gurdjieff was and is suspect if only for the reason that any teaching that is not, as it were, protected by general public or religious approval is suspect. We suspect what we cannot grasp immediately. Gurdjieff's own literary works have contributed to this "suspicion," being for the most part incomprehensible to the average reader. But to go back to Miss Mansfield:

---

1 All quotations are from *Katherine Mansfield's Letters to John Middleton Murry 1913-1922* Ed. by John Middleton Murry, Constable & Co., Ltd., London, 1951. The pages are given in each case. These quotations are reprinted by courtesy of the Society of Authors as the literary representative of the Estate of the late Katherine Mansfield.

"Mr. Gurdjieff is not in the least like what I expected. He's what one wants to find him, really. But I do feel *absolutely confident* he can put me on the right track in every way, bodily and t'other governor." (pp. 676-677)

"I believe Mr. Gurdjieff is the only person who can help me. It is great happiness to be here. Some people are stranger than ever, but the strangers I am at last feeling near, and they are my own people at last. So I feel. Such beautiful understanding and sympathy I have never known in the outside world." (p. 679)

"There is another thing here—Friendship. The real thing that you and I have dreamed of. Here it exists between women and women and men and women, and one feels it is unalterable, and living in a way it never can be anywhere else. I can't say I have friends yet. I am simply not fit for them. I don't know myself enough to be really trusted, and I am weak where these people are strong. But even the relationships I have are dear beyond any friendships I have known." (p. 684)

"Sometimes I wonder if we 'make up' Mr. Gurdjieff's wonderful understanding. But one is always getting a fresh example of it. And he always acts at precisely the moment one needs it. That is what is so strange..." (p. 695)

"But this place has taught me so far how unreal I am. It has taken from me one thing after another (the things never were mine) until at this present moment all I know really, really is that I am not annihilated and that I hope—more than hope—believe." (p. 698)

There is, of course, much more about Gurdjieff and the Institute in this book. I have failed to find anything in it that is "derogatory" to Gurdjieff. She does speak of the suffering and the difficulties which she encountered at the Institute from time to time but it seems to be impossible for any objective reader to conclude that Miss Mansfield did not welcome such experiences. They seemed to her to have real substance, purpose, and meaning.

In addition to Miss Mansfield's "testimony" on the subject of Gurd-jieff, there is a pertinent and interesting editorial note by John Middle-ton Murry at the conclusion of the same book:

"It is not for me to pass judgment on the Gurdjieff Institute. I cannot tell whether Katherine's life was shortened by her entry into it. But I am persuaded of this: that Katherine made of it an instrument for that process of self-annihilation which is necessary to the spiritual rebirth, whereby we enter the Kingdom of Love. I am certain that she achieved her purpose, and that the Institute lent itself to it. More I dare not, and less I must not say."

Whatever Mr. Murry's expressed intentions, surely this paragraph does pass judgment. And rather odd—or peculiar—judgment at that. For serious-minded people, entering the "Kingdom of Love" would not appear to be undesirable—in a sense, one might say it is the most desirable thing in the world; and the same comment could also be made about "spiritual rebirth." Which leaves us with the words "that process of self-annihilation." If "self-annihilation" is meant only as a means to "spiritual rebirth," etc., then I can only commend the process. If, on the other hand, Mr. Murry is suggesting (and the general tone of the quoted paragraph leads me to the conclusion that he is) that *physical* death was what Katherine Mansfield achieved—in other words, some form of suicide—then perhaps it should be questioned. Readers can—as a great many have—make their own conclusions about this.

But...Of course, there is a but. Katherine Mansfield was very seri-ously ill when she went to the Prieuré. Her relationship with her husband, Mr. Murry, had been, at least, "difficult" for a long time, as the *Letters* indicated. Even so, I can understand that Mr. Murry would not want his wife to die. On the other hand, had Katherine Mansfield been an old woman at the time of her death, I doubt that the veiled accusation—the implication that Gurdjieff and the Institute somehow contributed to her death, or became a helpful suicidal instrument—would have been made. The whole question, therefore, seems to me to come down to something rather simple: It was unfortunate, given our general conventional outlook on life, that Katherine Mansfield, a highly talented writer, died when she was so young.

Was it really so unfortunate? Can we regret the books that were never written? Can we regret the unlived life? Perhaps we can, logically, regret these things in the case of accidents—train wrecks, automobile crashes, murders. But it is doubtful that we can have such regrets even in the case of suicide which is, at least possibly, part of the victim's make-up and character. But, if Miss Mansfield did enter the "Kingdom of Love" and achieve "spiritual rebirth" (and, please note, Mr. Murry states "I am certain that she achieved her purpose"), then my only question would be: Was there anything else for her to achieve? Does anyone who ponders such questions have an alternative that is preferable? In fact, the statement of Mr. Murry can be taken as an extraordinary Christian tribute to Mr. Gurdjieff—one that I am not at all sure he deserves.

I am less convinced than Mr. Murry that Miss Mansfield "entered the Kingdom of Love" in the hereafter, which I assume is his implication. I do believe that her own testimony at least indicates that she found, not a kingdom, but a world of "friendship" and "reality" which had great meaning for her. No mean achievement.

In addition to the "testimony" of Miss Mansfield and of Mr. Murry, P. D. Ouspensky, who did not remain forever "taken in" by Gurdjieff, as his own books will testify, had this to say on the subject of Miss Mansfield and Gurdjieff:[2]

"I arrived at the Chateau Prieuré for the first time at the end of Octo-

---

2 Ouspensky, P.D. *In Search of the Miraculous: Fragments of an Unknown Teaching*. Routlege & Kegan Paul, London, 1950.

ber or the beginning of November, 1922.

"I remember one talk with Miss Katherine Mansfield who was then living there. This was not more than three weeks before her death. I had given her G.'s address myself. She had been to two or three of my lectures and had then come to me to say that she was going to Paris. A Russian doctor was curing tuberculosis by treating the spleen with X-rays. I could not of course tell her anything about it. She already seemed to me to be halfway to death. And I thought that she was fully aware of it. But with all this, one was struck by the striving in her to make the best use even of these last days, to find the truth whose presence she clearly felt but which she was unable to touch. I did not think that I should see her again. But I could not refuse when she asked me for the address of my friends in Paris, for the address of people with whom she would be able to talk about the things she had talked with me. And so I had met her again at the Prieuré. We sat in the evening in one of the salons and she spoke in a feeble voice which seemed to come from the void, but it was not unpleasant.

"'I know that this is true and that there is no other truth. You know that I have long since looked upon all of us without exception as people who have suffered shipwreck and have been cast upon an uninhabited island, but who do not yet know of it. But the people here know it. The others, there, in life, still think that a steamer will come for them tomorrow and that everything will go on in the old way. These already know that there will be no more of the old way. I am so glad that I can be here.'

"Soon after my return to London I heard of her death. G. was very good to her, he did not insist upon her going although it was clear that she could not live; For this in the course of time he received the due amount of lies and slander."

In my opinion, Mr. Ouspensky, regardless of any personal disagreement I had with him and despite the fact that his books are too "intellectual" for me, is one of the—if not *the*—most detached, objective critics of Gurdjieff, as witness his statement, in this same book:

"During this period G. invited me several times to go and live at the Prieuré. There was a good deal of temptation in this.

"At the same time I could not fail to see, as I had seen in Essentuki in 1918, that there were many destructive elements in the organization of the affair itself and that it had to fall to pieces."

In a final effort to be completely fair to Mr. Murry and to those who still assume that Mr. Gurdjieff "killed" Miss Mansfield, let us go back to the Prieuré and to Mr. Gurdjieff himself:

When I first worked at the Prieuré—in the stables—taking care of the horse and donkey, I was, as any child would have been, amused and interested by the narrow wooden staircase which led to a small platform above the stalls of the animals. There, on the ceiling over the low platform, were portraits of numerous birds and animals, all caricatures of Katherine Mansfield's friends at the Prieuré and painted, I was told, by Alexandre de Salzmann. As many of the same people who were caricatured were still students at the Prieuré, it amused me, too, to try to identify them. No one was willing to identify them for me. Also, childishly, it was entertaining to pretend to live the role of the invalid, lying on Katherine's narrow bed, smelling and hearing the animals below, and fantasying with the animal-likenesses above.

Even at the age of eleven, I had heard criticism of Gurdjieff along the lines of the "he killed Katherine Mansfield" accusation, and was greatly surprised to find all the older students, and Gurdjieff himself, speaking of her with great friendship, affection, and regret. Also, one of my first excursions outside the Prieuré grounds was with a number of my new-found friends to visit the grave of Katherine Mansfield in the small cemetery in Avon. I, for one, find it hard to believe that Katherine Mansfield could have been unhappy at the Prieuré. But that, of course, does not refute the possibility that Gurdjieff may have killed her. Gurdjieff at no time made any effort to dispel existing doubts about her death, and I assume that he was aware of the criticism. He did speak of her in my presence, but only as he would have spoken of a departed friend or relative—with affection and, it seemed to me, a good deal of "sentimentality."

I think I can say, fairly, that my position at the Prieuré was—at least to a great extent—unique. Unique in the sense that I had no "need" to be there. I was there, in fact, against my will—in the sense that any child is at a boarding school against his will—or at least, hardly by choice. Because of this, I regarded Mr. Gurdjieff as I might have observed anyone in authority. He was, in a general way, just another adult—with more or less the same powers that any headmaster would be expected to have. The only sense in which he seemed "unusual" was that he was treated with more awe and respect than is common among, shall we say, headmasters? If comparing Gurdjieff to a "headmaster" or to "any adult" seems "naïve" or "ridiculous," I can only say that Gurdjieff did not seem any more odd to me than, for example, Jane Heap, Margaret Anderson, Gertrude Stein, Brancusi, etc. More imposing, if you wish, but no odder.

The important point is, I think, that I had not come to the Prieuré *searching* for anything. Someone said, recently in my hearing: "Gurdjieff was for the misfits in life. He had some sort of system which appealed to the neurotic, the dissatisfied people who could not find any answers or any solace in religion, philosophy, and so forth." I have no particular quarrel with this statement. Most of the "followers" or habitués of the Prieuré were "misfits" in the sense that they were seeking some answer, some reason, and were dissatisfied with whatever had been available to them before encountering Gurdjieff. Since, as he explained constantly, dissatisfaction was practically essential for candidates for his method, I am hardly surprised.

As a child, I was not conscious of anything "unusual" about the Prieuré. While it apparently seems strange to people who have heard about Gurdjieff and his theories—life at the Prieuré did not fit in with their conceptions of what life must have been at an "Institute for the Harmonious Development of Man." Generally, at least for a child, life at the Prieuré was simple, even elemental, in the sense that our occupations had to do with growing food for our own use, keeping the place in order, and so on. To me, the students were something like a large body of caretakers and maintenance-men. We might easily have been called a corps of janitors, gardeners, or servants. My personal relationship with Mr. Gurdjieff, of course, made me aware that something more than "maintenance" work was going on—but the nature of that relationship was no more arresting or unusual than any child's relationship to an exceptional parent. He, Gurdjieff himself, was peculiar. But at that age most adults were peculiar in my eyes—and his peculiarities were only different in degree.

Also, the Prieuré was an outgoing, happy place for all children. Whatever torments may have been suffered by resident or visiting adults, they were not obvious to the children. We were treated—except by Gurdjieff—as children, and with a good deal of love, affection, and warmth. Unlike the other adults, Gurdjieff was the "boss" and, as such, entitled to exceptional behaviour and exceptional obedience. We thought of him as a kind of god—or perhaps an allpowerful king. Despotic, certainly, but also humorous, kind, affectionate, and frequently very funny. More than that—he seemed absolutely trustworthy and, to us, logical and right. If, at eleven, I could have understood what was supposedly taught at the Prieuré, I might have been baffled and confused. Since I didn't, I was only aware of being in a "good" place, with a good man. Unusual, if you wish, but so much the better. I had a natural child's respect for his unquestioned authority and for his eccentricities—they merely made him that much more interesting. Also he was unpredictable which, contrary to popular belief, was not at all frightening. It was far more stimulating than the activity of all the predictable adults. Although predictable, they were incomprehensible and rather boring: most adults are, a fact which seems to escape us except in childhood or in old age. But with Gurdjieff, we never knew what was going to happen next...and when it did, it was usually exciting and almost always amusing; sometimes he made it a magic world for children...imagine a man wild and wonderful enough to buy two hundred bicycles and make everyone ride them. What child could resist that alone?

If this digression seems over-long, may I justify it by stating that I have tried to give a picture of the Prieuré as I saw and knew it—as a child—about one year after Katherine Mansfield's death there. And to touch on that death once more, one important thing in the question was Gurdjieff's own attitude towards death itself. Mr. Murry may be quite right, in fact I think he is right, in at least part of his judgment about the Institute when he says that the "Institute lent itself to" her death-wish, as it were. Gurdjieff, obviously, did not place any great value on the prolongation of individual human life. His insistence upon the necessity to be constantly aware of the fact of one's death could be a dangerous thing for many people, of course. If the death-wish is as strong as some psychologists and doctors would have us believe, his insistence that one must "look it in the face" could strengthen that fertile wish. But such thinking fails to admit the perfectly obvious fact that everyone is going to die anyway, and why not admit that fact and live with it?

My opinion of Katherine Mansfield's end, partly from the letters and other opinions quoted previously, and partly from my knowledge of Gurdjieff and the Institute, is that she was—whether psychologically or physically—dying when she went to Gurdjieff for the first time. Someone other than Gurdjieff, and here is where I seem to be in agreement with Mr. Murry, might have made great efforts to save her life—or to prolong it. Gurdjieff would not have done that, and certainly, in my opinion, did not do it. But it would be hard for me to disagree with whatever it was that he did do. She died, or at least prepared for

death, in a more reconciled and "happier" state than she appeared to
have achieved before in her life. Who knows, definitely, that an acceptance—to some degree—of death, is not a desirable thing? I point out
again, that I had no personal experience with Miss Mansfield and was
not present at the time of her death—also that I am convinced that
Gurdjieff's "work" in her case was only to help her struggle towards a
"proper" death. Finally, let us not rob Miss Mansfield of her stature
as a human being and a writer, by assuming that she had no control
whatsoever in the months before her death. She chose to be there. Her
letters, if nothing else, are certainly not the letters of a woman who was
being gradually "killed."

XXIII

MOST OF THE CRITICISM OF Mr. Gurdjieff and his method is curiously vindictive and personal. It is difficult for me to understand this sort of criticism for the simple reason that it never seems to take into account that there could have been any sort of personal responsibility in relation to Gurdjieff. This possibility is usually dismissed, or at least avoided, by the statement, or the implication, that Gurdjieff was so "hypnotic" or so "compelling" (or that there was something in his work that made it irresistible) that people were unable to save themselves from him.

I certainly admit Gurdjieff's personal magnetism; on the other hand, he made it very difficult for most people to become group members. In one instance that I remember very clearly, Gurdjieff was approached by a middle-aged American couple for help. The man was partially paralysed, and it was implicit in their request for admission to the Prieuré that they hoped his "work" could do something about this condition. Gurdjieff made it eminently clear, in my presence, that no aspect of his work could possibly do anything about the actual physical condition of the man (except to help him to accept it), but he had no objection to their admission to the Prieuré as long as they understood that nothing there would in any way help or alleviate the paralysis. In fact, at the beginning of the interview, which took place at the Prieuré, he at first refused them permission to establish themselves there as students. It was only after he had made his conditions perfectly clear—concerning the physical ailment—that they were allowed to stay.

I got to know the couple very well during their stay there—I was thirteen at the time, and there was a period when I was assigned to the work of cleaning their rooms. This was unheard of—everyone else cleaned their own rooms—but the exception was made in their case, as a form of courtesy, since the man was confined to a wheelchair and his wife was almost always with him, pushing him around the grounds in order that he could at least observe, if not participate in, the work that was going on. They stayed at the Prieuré for about two months, as I remember, and the wife, particularly, seemed to feel that she was "getting something" from being there. I don't know how her husband felt about this. I do know that when they left the Prieuré, they announced (more accurately, she did) that they intended to continue with his work in New York—with the New York group.

It was about nine or ten years later when I saw these people again. They made a particular effort to find me. I was very surprised to hear from them, and very glad to see them—as a child I had liked them both. To my complete astonishment, when I did see them in New York, they spoke of Gurdjieff with enormous personal hatred in their voices. I was so startled that I could not say very much and did not know of any way to defend him. But I did listen to them both, and their long hateful harangue amounted to the fact that Gurdjieff was a "fake," a "charlatan," and a "devil," mostly because he had not done anything about the man's physical condition.

In my rather simple-minded way I tried to remind them that he had warned them, specifically, and in my presence, that there was nothing he could do about that condition, but I might as well have tried to reason with them in a foreign language. Hatred simply does not respond to reasoning. This was my first experience—in connection with Gurdjieff—in clashing head on with a totally emotional point of view; so emotional that reason was completely disregarded. I have come up against it since then on many, many occasions.

Why is it that even now, years after Gurdjieff's death, the prevailing criticism of him is so entirely emotional and so rarely based on any fact? To me it has come to underline Gurdjieff's own words about the "savagery" of what he called the "feeling" or "emotional" centre in man. In my own personal experience in the world, quite apart from Gurdjieff, I am continually appalled at the force of emotional reactions in people and at the weakness of their reasoning power in emotional situations. In the case of Gurdjieff, I do not think it was his magnetism or his power that was the cause of the confusion. I think it was the expectations of the people who came into contact with him. I know of almost no one who was able to approach him and evaluate him from a detached, thinking point of view. Even the seemingly impartial admirers (and how could they be impartial and also admire?) would sometimes be horrified and prejudiced against him because he was, in their view, "dirty" or "insanitary." I, of all people, having cleaned his room for two years as a child, knew he could be dirty and insanitary, by western standards, but it had no more effect on me than the fact that he was a certain age or a certain height. What did his sanitary habits have to do with his knowledge or his abilities as a teacher? When I have asked that question, the reply always seems to be that a great teacher is, of necessity, clean. This seems to me to be the equivalent of accepting Christianity after an investigation of the bathing habits of Jesus Christ. Or is "cleanliness next to Godliness" after all? And does that old saw actually refer to physical cleanliness?

I have said in this book that I have no particular desire to defend Mr. Gurdjieff, and I suppose that statement is not absolutely true, or at least not cut-and-dried. If there is an implied defence of him in this criticism of some of his followers and detractors, it is due to my impatience with the lack of impartial reasoning on the part of such people. They seemed to see—and then evaluate—Gurdjieff through the emotional mist of their desires or wants or hopes and never with clarity. Is it really all the fault of the teacher if a student does not get straight A's?

All that Gurdjieff had to offer, as far as I know, was a teaching that was based on a great many other teachings, that was not necessarily *new*. If there was any novelty in it, it was in his method of teaching. But, my question to his critics would have to be: What made it so difficult either to accept or reject him or his teaching? Why do they have to become so violently, emotionally involved with it? I admit, at once, that I was emotionally involved with Gurdjieff as a man, and that he had enormous influence on my life; but I am emotionally involved with practically anyone I have known well, so why should—or how could—Gurdjieff be an exception? And emotional involvement does not preclude my awareness of the fact that such-and-such a person may have habits or traits that I may dislike or of which I may even "disapprove." But is my approval or affection going to be based on my observation of such things? In fact, can I take it upon myself to *approve* of anyone?

Of course, I have emotional reactions to people. But such reactions do not have the slightest effect on their individuality, or the "totality" of such people. They exist, as they are, in whatever way they choose—or happen to be led—which is something I cannot alter, even if I should wish to do so. The only thing I can do is to accept or reject such people in a personal sense. Life seems to me to be a predatory business by its very nature, and if a person is not "useful" (in the sense that there is some mutual, valuable exchange—on *whatever* level) to another person, why have a relationship with such a person? Cold-blooded? If you wish, but isn't the very expression "cold-blooded" a purely emotional one? If it were possible, I would do practically anything for my fellow man (why not?), but this should not be taken as an "altruistic" statement. Altruism, itself, is often a questionable motive, and usually an emotional one. In my periods of "loving the world" and feeling "altruistic" I have found, to my sorrow, that there isn't anything I can do for anyone else anyway. Certainly not in any *helpful* sense. I can share their lives, but only as long as such sharing is a mutually profitable (or enjoyable, or rewarding) process. Is there another way to live with people?

XXIV

WHATEVER PROTESTATIONS I MAY HAVE made to the contrary, it is probably impossible for me to stand back, impartially, and evaluate my own experience with Gurdjieff. I became so involved in the life of the Prieuré and with him as a child that such an evaluation would amount to asking a fish how his life had been affected by living in the water. Even so, I will make an attempt.

First of all, it seems important to emphasize the fact that I was primarily involved with, and interested in, the individual man—not his teaching; at least not in an intellectual sense. On the other hand, I think it was impossible to be associated with him in any way and not be affected by whatever he was teaching—he embodied his teaching. If I am aware of any single, permanent result of Gurdjieff in myself, it is a consciousness of total paradox. The duality of man's nature (whether manifested in myself or in someone else) seems to be, thanks to Gurdjieff, a condition that I am never able to forget. The only simple example—and it is fairly complicated, at that—that I can give is that there seems to be a part of me which has never, and will never, grow up in the ordinary sense of those words. I attribute this to Gurdjieff because it seems to me that one of his aims was to encourage the retention of a certain child-like naïveté in people. In his own writings he speaks of the necessity of "being able to preserve intact both the wolf and the sheep" in one's self. Roughly translated, this process, in my opinion, amounts to preserving "credulity" (or "innocence" or "naïveté") at the same time as one acquires "experience" (or "worldliness" or "scepticism").

Gurdjieff often said that it was necessary to "have all illusion" and "all disillusion" in life, and when he first said it to me when I was still a child, I took it to mean that a given person must, eventually, destroy all his illusions. In the course of time, it has come to mean something else. It is not so much a description of a process, as I now see it, as a description of a state of being that must be sustained. If one can retain the ability to "have illusions" it is then possible, no matter how cynical one's intellect might have become, to experience life, and to approach people, with an extreme receptivity. It amounts to the retention in oneself of what might be called "total gullibility."

To put this on a more personal, and understandable, basis, I would say that I believe that everyone always tells the truth. Even when I know they are lying, I believe they are telling the truth. If this seems like a contradictory or paradoxical statement, I would point out that "believing" and "knowing" are two different things and should not be confused. The ensuing struggle—the conflict between belief and knowledge—within oneself becomes a means to an end which some-how produces an open mind and a path to "understanding" which lies somewhere between belief and knowledge. The value in it, for me, is that in the conflict I am forced to evaluate not only another person but, inevitably, myself. Thanks to just this process, I am *involved* in life, in other people.

If this process seems pointless, or inexplicable, there is very little I can say about it that will make it any clearer or give it any meaning. It seems to come down to the necessity of believing in people, *per se,* however they may happen to manifest themselves; and also continuing to rediscover the fact that life (or nature) is full of wonder—perma-nently startling.

One of the great difficulties in writing about Gurdjieff, or in trying to "explain" him, is that most people take him and his work so *seri-*

ously. Whether for or against him, they are seriously so. I suppose that the fundamental "seriousness" of the subject—how to perfect oneself into real manhood (or however one might wish to describe his work)—calls for a certain gravity. But, again paradoxically perhaps, Gurdjieff's strong belief in the "total" man and in the development of all facets of one's being, seems to me to presuppose that one must at the same time realize how ridiculous the whole process is. This "seriousness" which, in his disciples, often amounted to reverence, is the main reason that he has been the centre of controversy in those circles professing interest in him. His "philosophy" is, almost always, criticized as being "bogus" or "satanic," and defended as being a "true way," if not *the* true way. Somewhere in the controversy lies the apparently unnoticed or forgotten fact that Gurdjieff was, above everything, a *man*—in the perfectly ordinary sense that we are all men. As for his teaching, it was by his own admission based on various old and secret "teachings," and not invented by him. Also, by his own definition, he was a "troublemaker." Because of his personal struggles to keep his own duality alive—that duality and the resulting conflict which are apparently essential, in his view, to human progress—there must have been periods when he took himself too "seriously," too. Even so, he recovered, and his saving grace as a man and as a teacher, was his sense of humour with its resultant perspective.

While it is difficult to give any general examples of Gurdjieff's *method* of teaching, I do remember one instance which, when I think back on it, seems to me to embody a great many aspects of the manner in which he worked:

At one time, and as part of a general discussion on the "deterioration of knowledge and science" in the modern world, Gurdjieff brought up the subject of astrology. He claimed that many centuries ago it had been a "really genuine science" and very different from the present-day conception of astrology. As an example of the way in which it had been "civilized and misinterpreted" he said that the astrological signs were originally "invented" to synthesize the particular characteristics against which a given individual would have to fight—or to struggle—in the course of his life on earth.

He said that an individual born under the sign and influence of Aries, the Ram, should—properly—remember that the Ram was a symbol of the characteristics of his nature against which he should struggle in order to achieve harmony and balance within himself.

Scorpio, in this interpretation (the female kills the male when mating has been accomplished), could generally be interpreted as a "killing" sign, although he did not mean killing in a physical sense. He went on to point out that Pisces and Gemini were the two obvious dual signs, but that they represented two different kinds of duality. In Pisces, it is a warring duality—two fishes, tied together (as they are sometimes depicted in old engravings and drawings) but struggling to break the bond between themselves—in other words, Pisceans have to struggle against a self-divisive tendency in their own natures. Gemini, on the contrary, represented a merging duality, and the struggle was against ingrowingness and towards separation. Sagittarius has to struggle against destructiveness (the arrow aimed against the world)...and so on. The straightforward simple method being to find out what your sign symbolized in your mind and relate it to your natural characteristics.

Gurdjieff did not discuss all the signs in detail, but suggested that once one could discover, *for oneself*, what the sign symbolized or represented in the way of characteristics (or compulsions) in one's self, then one would have to remind oneself that such a synthesis represented those elements against which one would have to fight throughout life—what might be called the "built-in obstacles" in one's own nature that were part of the key to "self-perfection" or growth; the *necessary* obstacles standing in the path to development. He added that, as was usual in all great, ancient sciences, the lesson was never clearly stated, but could only be learned with effort, and that a great part of the problem in astrology was the individual's particular interpretation of the meaning of his sign for himself. Going back to Aries, as a convenient example, he said that it was not only that persons born under this sign would have to struggle against their tendency to "ram" (or batter) in various circumstances and situations, but that it would also depend upon their interpretation of "ramming" and their personal analysis and understanding of the ways in which this compulsive characteristic was manifested. The sign, in other words, was a key—an indication—for all persons born under it, but since each person differed individually, it would be necessary for them to find out for themselves in what particular ways the sign manifested in their individuality.

He warned that in the particular, individual search and analysis of such characteristics, a clue usually could be found if one was able to observe, objectively, the characteristics within oneself to which one is inordinately attached. He said that while it was very hard to observe one's personal prejudices and "pleasing characteristics" with real objectivity, it was nevertheless necessary to do so in order to evaluate oneself correctly. In this, other people could be useful, as through them it was possible to observe the effects (upon them) of one's own *recurring, individual* manifestations. One way to discover those things within ourselves to which we are attached, which we like and of which we are proud (although perhaps quite unconsciously), is the frequency of their repetition in outward manifestations—in dealings with other people. Such recurrent manifestations could be the first clue to our "vanities," which in turn should be interpreted in relation to the characteristics of our astrological sign.

In an attempt to give an easily comprehensible, hypothetical example, and a very obvious one, he said that if a given individual should observe that in his dealings with other people he manifested a certain, persistent, recurring insistence on "having his own way," and that such a person turned out to be someone who was born under the sign of Aries, the implication is fairly obvious. Learn how, consciously, not to insist. If a Piscean was also "insisting" in this sense, the insistence might be interpreted as a "one-sided" insistence; and it might be necessary to learn, consciously, to "insist" with the other half of one's nature.

If a person born under the sign of Aries can learn not to insist in his dealings with other people (assuming that he has found he does so), he will at least have learned the possibility of not being insistent in his own self-struggles towards growth or development. Any *recurring* manifestation (any unconscious habit) is, of necessity, a form of blindness in that the repetitive manifestation, by its very operation, prevents conscious activity.

In relating this rather general conversation to Gurdjieff's "work" or his "method" I could only conclude, personally, that it is a fairly clear example of his teaching—fundamentally, the discussion seemed to me to emphasize the need to produce constant struggle within oneself which, generally, was the basis of his method—anything to keep the pot boiling. Anything, including astrology.

The simplest guidepost that he gave in this discussion of astrology and the signs of the Zodiac was to watch for those things in oneself which one "loves"—whether they were physical, emotional, or mental manifestations, compulsions, habits, or characteristics (he gave a choice of terms). If you "loved" your hands as a physical feature—this was a clue of a kind; something to do with the use or function of the hands. If you "loved" or "cherished" your propensity for eloquence, this was another clue. If you loved or were proud of the fact that you were always "honest"...another clue. And so on. Not much in the way of answers, but as he admonished repeatedly, there are no answers except the ones that one finds for oneself.

As a concluding statement about Gurdjieff, as a teacher, I would say that he was, without question, fanatic in the sense that, however conscious he might have been, his sense of dedication to the dissemination of his method must necessarily be considered compulsive. (He gave his birthday as January 1, in case anyone wishes to practise astrology with that date in mind.) Considering him as compulsive, automatically produces a sense of paradox. His method was based on becoming "conscious" as opposed to being "led" or "pulled" or "compelled," and one is, therefore, logically forced to ask: Why then did he teach? Would a totally conscious man—conscious, for instance, of the fact that he could only fulfil—or solve—his own destiny (if that is possible)—devote his life to an attempt to teach others? I can only reiterate my conviction that he absolutely had to be a teacher, that he was, therefore, some sort of self-created, inevitable Messiah—which, it seems to me, finally brings him down to a very human level. However detached he may have been, how *involved* he must have been to *have to teach*.

Also, as if blindly drawn by some magnetic pull—some force larger than himself, his primary teaching activity, in the long run, was in America. This seems to me immensely suitable—where else is the search for God, for an authority, for guidance, so openly expressed, so desperately "needed"? There was real interest, of course, also in France and England, Germany and Russia, but it seems significant that, for the most part, his really ardent adherents are in the United States. *Seek, and ye shall find.* A teacher, as Gurdjieff would have been the first to point out, *needs* pupils. He seems to me to have done a unique piece of work for those who happened to *need* him. It was, obviously, a special need. Equally obvious, he was a "special" man. As a final quote from Gurdjieff himself: "Is very important to find proper vocation in life. Only in this way possible fulfil one's destiny." Unquestionably, he found the proper vocation, *for him.* I can only assume that he also fulfilled his destiny.

EPILOGUE

XXV

A FEW DAYS AFTER COMPLETING the preceding manuscript, I re-read, thanks to a fortuitous accident, the following passages from *Tertium Organum*:[3]

"In all living nature (and perhaps also in that which we consider as dead) *love* is the motive force which drives the creative activity in the most diverse directions.

"In springtime with the first awakening of love's emotions the birds begin to *sing*, and *build nests*.

"Of course a positivist would strive to explain all this very simply: singing acts as an attraction between the females and the males, and so forth. But even a positivist will not be in a position to deny that there is a good deal more of this singing than is necessary for 'the continuation of the species.' For a positivist, indeed, 'singing' is merely 'an accident,' a 'by-product.' But in reality it may be that this singing is *the principal function of a given species*, the realization of its existence, the purpose pursued by nature in creating this species; and that this singing is *necessary*, not so much to attract the females, as for some general harmony of nature which we only rarely and imperfectly sense.

---

3 P.D. Ouspensky, *Tertium Organum*. Routlege & Kegan Paul, London, 1951 (pp. 170-173).

"Thus in this case we observe what appears to be a collateral function of love, from the standpoint of the individual, may serve as a principal function of the species.

"Furthermore, there are no fledglings as yet: there is even no intimation of them, but 'homes' are prepared for them nevertheless. Love inspires this orgy of activity, and instinct directs it, because it is expedient from the standpoint of the species. At the first awakening of love this work begins. One and the same desire creates a new generation and those conditions under which this new generation will live. One and the same desire urges forward creative activity in all directions, brings the pairs together for the birth of a new generation, and makes them *build* and *create* for this same future generation.

"We observe the same thing in the world of men: there too love is the creative force. And the creative activity of love does not manifest itself in one direction only, but in many ways. It is indeed probable that by the spur of love, *Eros,* humanity is aroused to the fulfilment of its *principal function,* of which we know nothing, but only at times by glimpses hazily perceive.

"But even without reference to the purpose of the existence of humanity, within the limits of the knowable we must recognize that all the creative activity of humanity results from love. *Our* entire world revolves around love as its centre.

"Love unfolds in a human being traits of his which he never knew in himself. In love there is much both of the Stone Age and of the Witches' Sabbath. By anything less than love many men cannot be induced to commit a crime, to be guilty of a treason, to reanimate in themselves such feelings as they thought to have killed out long ago. In love is hidden an infinity of egoism, vanity and selfishness. Love is the potent force that tears off all masks, and men who run away from love do so in order that they may preserve their masks.

"If creation, *the birth of ideas,* is the light which comes from love, then this light comes from *a great fire.* In this eternally burning fire in which humanity and all the world are being incessantly purified, all the forces of the human spirit and of genius are being evolved and refined; and perhaps indeed, from this same fire or by its aid a new force will arise which shall deliver from the chains of matter all who follow where it leads.

"Speaking not figuratively, but literally, it may be said that love, being the most powerful of all emotions, unveils in the soul of man all its qualities patent and latent; and it may also unfold those *new* potencies which even now constitute the object of occultism and mysticism—the development of powers in the human soul so deeply hidden that by the majority of men their very existence is denied.

"In love the most important element is *that which is not,* which *absolutely* does not exist from the usual worldly, materialistic point of view."

Not only do these words of Ouspensky's strike a deeply responsive chord in me—they have the ring of final truth—they also explain, to me, the causes of the conflict that at one time existed between Ouspensky and Gurdjieff. When Ouspensky was first interested in Gurdjieff's "ideas," Gurdjieff told him that if he, Gurdjieff, "knew as much" as Ouspensky, he would be a very great teacher indeed. The statement seemed to me a puzzling one, even after Gurdjieff had explained to me many times that "knowledge is a *passing* presence."

While Ouspensky knew, in his mind, that "Love is the potent force that tears off all masks, and men who run away from love do so in order that they may preserve their masks," Gurdjieff *understood* it. The difference between knowledge and understanding, in our time, is something akin to the difference between knowing how to make a hydrogen bomb and using it. Gurdjieff used everything he knew because he understood what he knew. Ouspensky, in a comparative sense, could only communicate on an intellectual level—his books, as reading, are far more interesting and readable than any book Gurdjieff has ever written. This fact, however, does not automatically give them more *content*.

There may be many of Gurdjieff's "disciples" who could, or do, feel, that they have been maligned by my recollections of Gurdjieff's life. I am not apologizing to them for my observations of their behaviour—the behaviour of human beings under the impact of an unquestionably extraordinary human being who *loved* them is not predictable, nor is it important.

What I *knew* as a child, I am beginning to *understand* as an adult. Gurdjieff *practised* love in a form that is unknown to almost everyone: without limits.

In the Gurdjieffian sense, "to be or not to be" is not a soul-searching question. It is a preliminary statement concerning a necessary decision. Having known Gurdjieff, there is only one possible answer and, therefore, no question at all.

AFTERWORD

AFTERWORD

By Alexandra Carbone, Managing Editor of
The Fritz Peters Collection

Documentarian of *On the Fritz*

WHY FRITZ? WHY NOW?

Because stories are not book reports. They are concentrated potions of experience. A quality story induces catharsis and understanding—a way to get more life out of life, to gain a wider view. Like Fritz Peters' *Boyhood with Gurdjieff,* our point of departure.

When we read the memoir years ago, we wanted to see Fritz mow lawns and make trouble on the big screen. Seeking out his other works, we discovered deeply personal stories about compelling times and places. The complex characters and paradoxical truths jump off the page and walk with the reader. We found classics – ahead of their time and falling out of print – so we embarked on a mission at Vanitas Vanitatum to republish Fritz Peters' books, to make a documentary about him, and to adapt his books into movies. What you hold in your hands is the first step.

Life And Work

The themes seem disparate, but they coalesce in one person. Mental illness. Homosexuality. Spirituality. Military service. Death drive.

Nonconformism. The war of the sexes. The self and society. Work. Fritz wrote about them because he knew them; in fact, could not escape them, had something he had to say about them, something to get off his chest. The books are highly personal, highly autobiographical. Multiple friends of his reported that "He only wrote when he had a book in him," and when he did the writing would come out in a mad rush, "sometimes in only a couple weeks."

Fritz lived from 1913-1979. Born in Wisconsin, he spent much of his turbulent youth in France, interacting with remarkable people operating at a frontier of human experience. People like his mentor and father figure, G.I. Gurdjieff, and his aunt, Margaret Anderson— plus the gaggle of avant-garde greats in her milieu. Fritz learned that words and thoughts were a path to social standing and self-respect. "He was brilliant, talented. He hung out with e.e. cummings and D.H. Lawrence. He enjoyed the fame he got, but I think he wanted to be a big star," said his daughter, Katharine Rivers.

It is difficult to define a person, even in hindsight, since people are developing stories. But by midlife, Fritz's best writing was behind him. His memoirs *Boyhood with Gurdjieff (1964)*, and *Gurdjieff Remembered (1965)*, are the exception. His literary career after *The Descent (1952)* mostly amounted to rejected manuscripts and burned bridges. In the mid-1960s, a reader at Farrar Straus scrawled, "I doubt that the manuscript will get anywhere—it is so obviously [close to/or] psychotic. The poor bastard has had (and has given others) an awful life. I am not hopeful that anything will result."

Succumbing To His Demons

"He had a death wish, he was drinking himself to death," said Fritz's friend, psychologist Barbara Vacarr, of his last decade of life. Cirrhosis was noted on his death certificate. At the close of World War II, his mentor, mystic and healer G. I. Gurdjieff, recognized the delicacy of Fritz's condition and recommended that he drink, but "consciously"...

> He insisted that I had such a need, but that it was periodic, and predicted that if I gauged the need properly I would go through periods where I would drink—or would need to drink—a good deal, and also sometimes through long periods when I would not need to drink at all; in fact, at such times, I would find that liquor might even be harmful for me.[4]

Gurdjieff implies that alcohol was a way to modulate Fritz's erratic moods, and probably anesthetize painful memories, but finding the prescribed balance proved perilous.

Mental illness has a nature and nurture component, both at play in Fritz's development. His childhood amounted to mitigated orphanhood due to his parents' divorce and his mother's nervous breakdowns. His mother remarried multiple times, selecting husbands who were not safe or did not want Fritz and his brother Tom present. Fritz preferred the care of Margaret Anderson, his maternal aunt, and her partner Jane Heap—largely so he could live at Gurdjieff's Institute. However, there were skeletons in that closet. This graphic episode that Fritz recounted in 1978 occurred when he was 11 years old. His disconnected, almost blasé attitude about it makes one wonder what other horrors he experienced:

> The final so-called disaster occurred when Jane [Heap], in a fit of anger...struck me with a board from a crate with nails in it.

---

4 Fritz Peters, *Gurdjieff Remembered* (Los Angeles: Hirsch Giovanni Publishing, 2021), 83.

Jane lost that one (or I won it, depending on how you look at it) because although the nails went all the way into my back and I was bleeding, I did not break down, cry, or otherwise participate in the scene. Jane was more than contrite, fell to her knees, hugged me, and begged for my forgiveness. I think that was the first time that my born 'rage to live' turned into active hatred. I told her that I would not only not forgive her—it was 'not my province' was one of the things that I said—but I told her that I would get even. I regret, in the long run, to have to admit that I did. On the same compulsive, unconscious, dreary level.[5]

His first novel, *The World Next Door (1949)*, shows how "succumbing to one's demons" in this manner, can be an oversimplification. As the novel unfolds in vivid stream-of-consciousness, we see that severe mental illness is not a sick spell that occurs in the context of a healthy mind, akin to a head cold. Instead, it is a state of confusion that overtakes a person who is a tenuous arrangement of wholeness; so, wholeness cannot be maintained over an extended stretch of life, with all its inherent hardships. Fritz explores the connection between alcohol and mental illness in this striking passage:

Only the liquor, a thin hot stream inside me, dripped like fuel to the last ember of warmth and light between my ribs, and fought the darkness. But there is another light beginning now: a light that does not warm, but reveals and distorts. In this light, pallor becomes sickness, and sickness, death. As the darkness itself had spread like the moving blotch of blood upon bright cloth, so this light penetrated the darkness.[6]

5 Fritz Peters, *Balanced Man* (London: Wildwood House, 1978), 62.

6 Fritz Peters, *The World Next Door* (Los Angeles: Hirsch Giovanni Publishing, 2021), 10.

When Fritz lost control of his mental state, on an extreme of what was then called manic depression, there would be no "Fritz" there to manage the alcohol, or moods, or work, or parenting, or other relationships. He would not know he was so compromised, and often neither would those closest to him. *Fig. 1* summarizes the periods of instability during Fritz's most productive decade of writing, much of which became fuel for his fiction. He recuperated in a mental hospital after his breakdown in 1958, during which he stared into the sun and claimed to be the second coming, just like the protagonist in *The World Next Door (see Fig 2)*. Forced to admit Fritz would never be a safe caretaker to their children, Jean Peters initiated divorce proceedings.

Fritz's ability to inhabit healthy and imbalanced states and communicate them to readers is one of his most illuminating transmissions—one for which he paid dearly. It would be an understatement to say that Fritz was a difficult person to live with and love. Though he was rarely single, his relationships were volatile and tended to end in explosions, if not mental breakdowns. This is perhaps why relationships—the ways in which they are doomed and the reasons they are inevitable—are what Fritz found most inspiring to write about. He distilled relationships into the heartbreaking truth that is the lifeblood of literature.

The World Next Door

The World Next Door is about a mental patient's relationship with himself, his medical staff, and his family. It examines everyone's interests and self-interest, as they scrap for dominance in the bureaucracy of a VA mental ward. Though highly autobiographical, it would be naive to take David Mitchell's words entirely at face value—he was, after all, suffering from paranoid delusions. Conversely, David Mitchell did not leave the VA Hospital against medical advice, whereas Fritz's former wife reports that he did *(see Fig. 1)*. Still, the novel speaks unflinchingly about how it feels to go through electro-shock and other crude techniques of early psychiatry, about cruelty from overburdened attendants, about a post-war government insti-tution that cared for some of its veterans (white, straight) better than others (black, gay).

In *The World Next Door,* the protagonist is conflicted about his homosexual inclinations. He claims not to prefer the company of men—he does not, therefore, identify as homosexual. However, he asserts the naturalness of his homosexual relationship: "I was in love with him, that's all."[7] Societal context makes this stance understand-able, yet revolutionary. This is because mental illness, discrimination, and homosexuality were linked in the context of a VA mental ward in the late 40s, much more deeply than today's reader might expect.

At the dawn of World War II, the U.S. military planned to cull any recruits at high risk for mental illness—prone to "shellshock," and costly disability payments. Psychiatry as a discipline was in its infancy, so the military added rounds of psychiatric testing to the physical screening process. After World War I, "The U.S. Govern-ment spent more than a billion dollars to treat mental casualties, and it was widely recognized that the government had a responsibility to avoid a huge loss of men and money in the next war."[8]

In 1941, the category of "Homosexual proclivities" was specifically identified as a form of mental illness incompatible with military

---

7 Peters, *The World Next Door,* 190.

8 Naoko Wake, "The Military, Psychiatry, and 'Unfit' Soldiers, 1939-1942," Journal of the History of Medicine and Allied Sciences 62, no. 4 (January 4, 2007): 466, https://doi. org/10.1093/jhmas/jrm002.

Fig 1

His periods of disturbance (or, as we referred to them, his "manic" periods) are repetitive and cyclic. As far as I have been able to determine, after talking to his mother,(his former wife and a very close friend of his, the following disturbed periods occurred:

1945 two hospitalizations in Army hospital in France

1947 committed to Lyons VA Hospital in N.J. for 3 months, released "against medical advice".

1950 suicide attempt and subsequent hospitalization in Clinton, N.Y., after manic period of 3-4 months.

1953 automobile accident and hospitalizationfollowing manic period lasting from February to October.

1954 severe automobile accident after manic period of 1-2 months, around early summer.

1955 beginning period in May that decreased following our marriage in June.

1956 brief, but intense period following birth of our daughter in April, and another brief and not too intense period in August-September.

1957 June to November period, very intense in August then in October.

1958 December to February 9th commitment. Acute.

Fig. 2

Then, on January 17th, we moved. That morning he was completely irrational and unreasonable. Any differing of even trivial opinion caused a furious reaction from him. He took off his glasses and "looked into the sun"---which is indicative of the degree of his disturbance. (As described in World Next Door, in fact this was just like the book). His talking was incessant and highly erratic, but, as always, maintaining a certain logic, i.e., he would, after many and lengthy digressions, always return to his original point. During this time he spoke of his being the second coming of Christ, of going to the sun, etc.

Excerpts From a letter from Fritz's wife, Jean R. Peters to his Psychologist, Dr. St. Pierre, at the VA Hospital in Topeka Kansas, in 1958

(Fig. 1) We see how Fritz struggled with instability even in his most successful decade of writing. Elements from his novels are present, such as the suicide attempt in *Finistère* (1951), and the car crash in *The Descent (1952)*.

(Fig. 2) *The World Next Door (1949)* is more directly autobiographical, as his wife Jean attested in further notes about his 1958 breakdown.

service by the advisory board to the military psychiatrists running the screening process. Homosexual behavior was deemed a form of sexual deviancy and a pre-psychotic state.[9] Many recruits with homosexual proclivities desired to join the war effort, however, and managed to avoid detection.

At the end of World War II, the U.S. Military hunted down and dishonorably discharged these homosexual soldiers. Gay service-men found guilty of sodomy were incarcerated, as it was illegal, and lesbian soldiers were also targeted. A dishonorable discharge rendered these soldiers ineligible for benefits, and they suffered some-times serious indignities in the process. At worst, they were held in impromptu brigs, in prisoner-of-war conditions, possibly sexually assaulted, even, by their own captors.[10] This phenomenon is echoed in *The World Next Door* when David Mitchell has an experience of being sexually coerced by an attendant in the VA hospital. For those homosexual soldiers lucky enough to be stationed where the U.S. Army ejected them under less inhumane conditions, the outcome was still damaging. A diagnosis would be placed on the gay soldier's discharge papers which could out them as homosexual.

If a diagnosis was listed on the discharge papers, the soldiers would be associated with a mental illness that sounded severe. "Psychotic personality" was one such label.[11] Anyone looking at their records could see the reason for their discharge—such as potential employers who requested military records for job applications. Homosexuals who managed to be hired were not secure in their offices, either.

9 Wake, "The Military, Psychiatry, and 'Unfit' Soldiers, 1939-1942," 476.

10 For first-hand accounts of this see *Coming Out Under Fire*, directed by Arthur Dong (1994; New York: Deep Focus Productions, Inc).

11 Wake, "The Military, Psychiatry, and 'Unfit' Soldiers, 1939-1942," 485.

Thousands of homosexual employees were purged from Federal positions during the Lavender Scare of McCarthyism, under discriminatory practices which persisted in the following decades.[12]

It is difficult to know how these policies affected Fritz during his short stint in the military, since he was justifiably mentally ill enough to be hospitalized and was honorably discharged. This context explains, however, why the medical staff was aware of David Mitchell's gay relationship in *The World Next Door*, and why the flirtation with the gay General was such a delicate matter. It explains why it was so difficult for Fritz and doctors to separate his sexuality from his mental illness. It also explains the stakes of going straight, and how confusing the situation must have been for a man with homosexual leanings, and manic depression, who was also attracted to women. A post-war reader would know this background, and perceive the hidden currents it creates in the storyline.

On the psychiatric side, as Fritz describes in *The World Next Door*, homosexuals tended to be well-behaved patients and many doctors treated them sympathetically; doctors had bigger problems on a mental ward. However, sympathy has its limits in the context of the pathologization of one's sexuality. Homosexuals of the time had difficulty navigating their mental health problems, especially if they refused to renounce their sexuality. Ed Field had such an experience with a doctor "who immediately decided that my homosexuality was at the root of all my miseries, and set out to change me."[13]

---

12 Suyin Haynes, "You've Probably Heard of the Red Scare, but the Lesser-Known, Anti-Gay 'Lavender Scare' Is Rarely Taught in Schools," *TIME* magazine, December 22, 2020, https://time.com/5922679/lavender-scare-history/.

13 Edward Field, afterword to *Finistère*, by Fritz Peters (Vancouver: Arsenal Pulp Press, 2006), 333-34.

Homosexuality would not be completely de-pathologized, removed from the Diagnostic Statistician's Manual (along with any loophole that enabled billing insurance for conversion therapy), until "ego-dystonic homosexuality" was removed in 1987.[14] This was after years of gay activism and vitriolic national debates. It would be three more decades before homosexuals earned an uncloseted place in the military, in 2011. Accordingly, Fritz's first-hand account of attitudes towards homosexuality, and the realities of homosexual soldiers on the VA mental ward, in post-war America, is compelling reportage relevant to both U.S. and Queer history.

The World Next Door impressed the medical community in 1949 and was carried in psychiatric libraries. They valued it because it was a unique first-hand account of what a severely ill patient experiences on a mental ward. Timely and bold, it also struck a nerve with post-war readers. "Not so much composed as forced out of the writer by the need to put down a terrible experience while still raw and quivering from its impact," wrote Antonia White, in *New Statesman*. With its experimental treatment of such gritty subject matter, Peters' autobiographical novel was critically well-received on the literary front and Fritz was lauded as a young writer to watch.

Finistère

"I loved *Finistère* because it was a beautiful love story. It showed Fritz's tenderness and the connection at the place where you could see his soul," said Barbara Vacarr.

Finistère, published only two years after *The World Next Door*, is a

14 Jack Drescher, "Out of DSM: Depathologizing Homosexuality," *Behavioral Sciences (Basel)* 5, no. 4 (December 4, 2015), Page 565, https://www.ncbi.nlm.nih.gov/pmc/articles/PMC4695779/.

coming-of-age, coming-out story about a teen's love affair with the tennis coach at his French boarding school. It is Fritz Peters' most successful book, still relevant today as a landmark novel of queer literature. So much ground has been won for queer rights over the past century, and so many aspects of gender have been redefined, that the current mood is to be reflective about the past while envisioning the future. *Finistère*'s themes of confusion, isolation, and self-destruction in the face of intolerance are, sadly, still applicable to queer teens today. But *Finistère* also celebrates love's ability to blossom where it is required, and it portrays love as an instinctive tropism toward healing and hope. It is thus a pioneering gay paean as much as it is a classic romance relevant to anyone who loves.

Finistère would not be art if it did not ask difficult questions and reveal uncomfortable truths. Today's readers are, hopefully, dismayed that the lovers in *Finistère* are so far apart in age. Michel is in his late 20s, and Matthew is only a teen. Upon opening the book to read, this writer was concerned the material might be handled inappropriately. Closing the book, those concerns were allayed. *Finistère*, with all its controversial aspects, provides valuable insight into the field of human experience.

It is perhaps unavoidable to compare *Finistère* to Nabokov's *Lolita*. *Lolita* is also a classic, adapted to film amid controversy. Readers find its age gap scandalous. However, Humbert Humbert, the narrator of *Lolita*, has a predilection for young ladies and premeditatively targets girls without remorse. He marries Lolita's mother to get closer to the object of his desire. Humbert is, simply put, a pedophile. On the contrary, Michel is a gay man who is uncomfortable with older/younger affairs, even though they were accepted by his peers in 1920s Paris. Michel broke with his long-term lover when the latter engaged in an encounter with an adolescent, the last straw after multiple infidelities. Heartbroken and disgusted, Michel accepts a teaching position that his father arranges. Michel is relieved to escape the excesses of Paris and has abandoned all hope for love. Suppressing his sexual impulses entirely—"vows of chastity, purity, reform"[15]—seems the best course of action. Matthew, though younger, initiates and directs the affair. Such details mitigate Michel's questionable behavior as much as possible. Many readers will likely react with moral disgust anyway, condemning Michel, opining that as the superior, Michel should have drawn a line—should not have engaged in any physical encounter with a student. Michel could have waited, they might say, if the two really loved each other. That perspective is valid.

However, relationships like Matthew and Michel's happen, and they happen for a reason. *Finistère* faces this reality. Why did it happen in this case? Why was it doomed? Does that mean such relationships are always doomed? Would Matthew have survived to adulthood with nobody to love him? If Michel had loved Matthew better, would their affair still have ended in tragedy? Was it possible for Michel to love Matthew better? What family and societal contexts contributed to the outcome? How would you feel if you read it as a teenager? Would you feel differently if you read it as a parent? Have you ever done anything unwise for love? Saying Michel should have drawn a line is like saying Othello should have ignored Iago. Pondering controversial situations in stories develops wisdom and compassion, fostering better decisions in the real world. That has always been the utility of tragedy.

Finistère feels too closely observed to be invented, but due to the covert nature of the relationship, it is unclear to whom it refers. Even the dedication to the novel is an enigma: "For A.P.S. and L.S.B.S 1900-1950." Enigma invites conjecture. It is the only dedication Fritz

---

15 Fritz Peters, *Finistère*, (Los Angeles: Hirsch Giovanni Publishing, 2021), 146.

writes that does not use full names. A person born in 1900 would be thirteen years older than Fritz (born Arthur Peters), roughly the age gap in the novel. A person who died in 1950 would have passed while Fritz was writing *Finistère*. Fritz attended boarding school in France for short periods of time, though he never graduated high school nor worked as a teacher.

When Fritz wrote *Finistère* he was in his late thirties and married to *Harper's Bazaar* fiction editor, Mary Lou Aswell. Fritz dedicated *The World Next Door* to Mary Lou, "without whom this book would not have been written." Aswell also had an interest in mental illness; she edited a book titled *The World Within (1947)*, shortly before meeting Fritz, which is a collection of "fiction illuminating the neuroses of our time." She fostered the careers of many homosexual writers in *Bazaar*'s pages, including Truman Capote. Ed Field, (Fritz's friend, gay poet and World War II veteran) reported that what Fritz wrote depended on the relationship he was in at the time, so it seems that Mary Lou was Fritz's most effective muse.

Aswell would go on to partner with sculptor Agnes Sims, her first same-sex lover, and Fritz dedicated his next novel, *The Descent*, to Agnes. The two women moved to Santa Fe, where their household was openly possible. One of the most affecting dynamics in *Finistère* is the impossibility for same-sex relationships to endure in a culture that is so intolerant of them. Although the current fashion bends toward feel-good LGBTQ stories, it is also important to understand the necessity of societal support to provide a framework for lasting relationships. In *Finistère* the "problem" was not the homosexuality, it was the intolerance. It is this perspective that made *Finistère* so pioneering. Threatened by Matthew's naivete, Michel remarks, "I suppose there's no reason why you should be able to understand that your happiness is something the world would think of as ugly and horrible and unnatural. But they do and I guess you'll learn soon enough."[16]

The *New York Times* review echoed this sentiment, saying "So far as this reviewer recalls, this is the best novel he has ever read on the theme of homosexuality (Proust excepted) and its tragic consequences in a world made up of 'selfish, ruthless, cruel, egocentric people.'"[17] Ed Field agreed: "*Finistère* is a marvelous book. It was the first gay novel I read, the rest were pulp."

The Descent

During the breakup of his marriage to Mary Lou, at the close of 1950, Fritz stood on the side of the highway interviewing motorists in upstate New York. He was working on his next novel, *The Descent*. If *Finistère* is a novel about why homosexual relationships cannot work, *The Descent* is a novel about why heterosexual relationships cannot work. We see couples poisoned by gender norms; the desire to dominate and be dominated poisoning Henry and Mabel, the cycle of lust and shame poisoning Caroline and Tom, the projections of male inadequacy poisoning Richard and Dorothy.

At the time Fritz operated in society as a heterosexual, but he always had male lovers. Fritz writes female characters remarkably well for a male writer, inhabiting them in a manner that only someone who has been an object of male desire can. He has an objective, almost anthropological eye to gender relations. Doris Hart, the hospital admin from *The Descent*, exemplifies this when she casts off the desire for validation from her patronizing, patriarchal psychologist. "What

---

16 Peters, *Finistère*, 155.

17 Herbert F. West, "Deep Water — And Black," *New York Times*, February 18, 1951, https://www.nytimes.com/1951/02/18/archives/deep-water-and-black.html.

was it that Dr. Cramwell had written? 'Psychological problems?' 'Primeval female sexual manifestations?' It was all a lot of nonsense. And why was she spending ten hard-earned dollars an hour to go to him?"[18]

Doris Hart's reverie continues on a slightly different track, "She thought of her husband with curious unexpected tenderness. If she stopped going to Dr. Cramwell, he'd be able to afford a new suit. And she might, eventually, be able to afford a television set." *The Descent* is also a portrait of post-war America and its hyperactive consumer-conformism, playing out in intimate relationships. This conformism was itself a veneer over societal divisions and war trauma—exemplified by the character of Jim Curran, the troubled war veteran. How can veterans relate to those who stayed home, and vice versa? How can men and women bridge the gender gap? Another return to normalcy. Do we all realize how normal it is to feel unfulfilled? What is the American Dream's answer to that? Where are we all going, so fast?

A tightly written suspense novel with a *Twilight Zone* feel, *The Descent* was well-received. However, Fritz could not know the turn his life was about to take. He would not publish again for twelve years. After finishing *The Descent*, Fritz fell into a long-term relationship with a man for the first time, Santa Fe-based painter Cady Wells. Fritz thought Cady was "the one," but it ended in volatile fights:

> Although Cady was enraptured with Fritz, his friends found Peters threatening and hateful, and he was a deeply disturbed man (he apparently once tried to kill Cady with a knife).

---

18 Fritz Peters, *The Descent* (Los Angeles: Hirsch Giovanni Publishing, 2021), 255.

Another of Peters' lovers, the painter William Brown, explained that each time Peters had a homosexual love affair he would rebound from it by marrying.[19]

Cady died soon after their split, of a heart attack, and Fritz headed into family life, marrying Jean. As *The Descent* foretold, and as already discussed, family life was not a good fit. After their divorce, Fritz moved to New York and finally found a stable relationship, by Fritz's standards, with painter Lloyd Goff. He seemed more at peace living as a gay man, according to his daughter. He sent money home for the children and kept in contact via frequent letters, phone calls, gifts, and occasional visits. He finally attempted writing again. His U.K. publisher, Victor Gollancz, encouraged him to write memoirs. Fritz published *Boyhood with Gurdjieff* in 1964, for which Henry Miller wrote the preface, saying "I regard it as something on a par with *Alice in Wonderland*, a real treasure of our literature."[20] Although it was a critical success followed by a sequel, *Gurdjieff Remembered* (1965), in terms of sales the memoirs found only a niche. *The World Next Door* was recorded for French radio and there were references, in Fritz's letters to Farrar Straus, to film deals that never solidified. He attempted writing novels again, and the rejections hit hard. He harangued Farrar Straus to republish his earlier novels or else revert the rights to him. Fritz was soon short on cash, began drinking more and more heavily and took on a seedy appearance. At the start of the 70s, Fritz headed back to Santa Fe, began a new novel, and published a final essay about Gurdjieff.

19 Lois P. Rudnick, "Under the Skin of New Mexico: The Life, Times, and Art of Cady Wells," in *Cady Wells and Southwestern Modernism*, ed. Lois P. Rudnick (Santa Fe: Museum of New Mexico Press, 2009), 71.

20 Henry Miller, preface to *Boyhood with Gurdjieff*, by Fritz Peters (Santa Barbara: Capra Press, 1980), Page ii.

Although Gurdjieff had died some 30 years earlier, Fritz spent his last days remembering the man and what they had meant to each other.

Gurdjieff — Father Figure And Guru

Gurdjieff had a powerful personality and a magnetic aura; it was easy for him to attract seekers to learn the esoteric wisdom he had accumulated. A mainstay of the philosophy at his *Institute for the Harmonious Development of Man* was that people go through life "asleep," so precious few develop themselves anywhere near their capacity. This is due to a failure to "do the work"—people lack the knowledge and focus to develop their various "centers." The "centers" are the Intellectual, Emotional, and Physical modes of being. These centers operate individually and together, creating new processes, requiring many types of "work" to exercise them all. Gurdjieff even called his teachings, "The Work." Confronting the real world, and all the obstacles one must overcome to finish a job, was one way to "wake up." This was chop-wood-carry-water spirituality, involving tasks like cooking, gardening, roofing, lawnmowing. Music and dance held a special role in the curriculum. Gurdjieff also employed flamboyant tricks, like pranks, to incite friction between people, launching them headfirst into healing crises. Dealing with the "unpleasant manifestations of others" leads to self-awareness and growth. Therefore, Gurdjieff appreciated Fritz's diligence, as much as his aptitude for mischief:

> Gurdjieff laughed, "What you not understand," he said, "is that not everyone can be troublemaker, like you. This important in life—is ingredient, like yeast for making bread. Without trouble, conflict, life become dead. People live in status quo, live only by habit, automatically, and without conscience. You good for Miss Madison. You irritate Miss Madison all time—more than

anyone else, which is why you get most reward. Without you, possibility for Miss Madison's conscience fall asleep.[21]

Putting Gurdjieff's practices in parable form is what Fritz achieves in *Boyhood with Gurdjeff*, in the direct style of Gurdjieff's teaching. As Gurdjieff's personal assistant, Fritz had an intimate view of the goings-on in the Institute. Gurdjieff appreciated Fritz's interest in philosophy and psychology, saying that Fritz was a "trash can" for Gurdjieff to "dump" his teaching into. What probably made Fritz so empty is that he had been abandoned by his family. He needed a trustworthy adult who could direct his curiosity and his stubborn streak. Fritz would never shake Gurdjieff's influence and would always work to digest it – Gurdjieff's ideas pervade Fritz's writing. Though Fritz read voraciously, he never finished high school nor attended college. Gurdjieff's Institute was his education, the stories he walked with and measured against. Michael Vacarr, Fritz's friend explained:

> Fritz said Gurdjieff saved his life. He was the only adult who made sense to him. Could Gurdjieff have saved his brother's life? I don't know. There was something Fritz brought to the situation with Gurdjieff that allowed Fritz to benefit from it. And Gurdjieff didn't let Fritz get lost in feeling sorry for himself.

Shortly before his death in 1949, Gurdjieff enacted an impactful prank-teaching, when he made an announcement at a gathering of students that Fritz attended. As Fritz recounts it, Gurdjieff said:

21 Fritz Peters, *Boyhood with Gurdjieff* (Los Angeles: Hirsch Giovanni Publishing, 2021), 170.

'In life is only necessary for man to find one person to whom can give accumulation of learning in life. When find such receptacle, then is possible die.' He smiled, benevolently, and went on: 'So now two good things happen for me. I finish work and I also find one person to whom can give results my life's work.' He raised his arm again, started to move it, this time with a finger extended and pointing, around the room, and then stopped when his finger was pointing directly at me. There was an enormous silence in the room and Gurdjieff and I looked at each other fixedly, but, even so, I was aware that one or two of the others had turned to look in my direction. The tension in the atmosphere did not lessen until Gurdjieff dropped his arm, turned, and left the room.[22]

Fritz would struggle with the mantle of chosen successor for the rest of his life. Gurdjieff's motivations for announcing this were mysterious, and Fritz thought of a few explanations. First, it might be "actually true." Second, it might be intended to "expose" Fritz's "massive ego" to himself—this was the preferred explanation of many Gurdjieff followers. Third, perhaps it was "a huge joke on the devout followers."

There is a special irony in selecting a person with a Messiah Complex to be one's "true successor." It is even possible Gurdjieff was making a joke at his own expense. Whatever the case, Fritz was "moved, confused, and perplexed" by the event.[23] Fritz would spend the rest of his days causing fuss and friction at Gurdjieff meetings and claiming to be the true successor, whether he truly believed it or not.

---

22 Peters, *Gurdjieff Remembered*, 90-91.

23 Peters, *Gurdjieff Remembered*, 93.

Why Fritz?

Fritz was more human than most. With internal and external experiences so extreme, he encountered the range of human experience in a way most people do not. There has always been a link between manic depression and creativity, perhaps because it is difficult to communicate peak experiences without resorting to art. In person Fritz could be charming, present, helpful, and funny—also irascible, inappropriate, inebriated, and exhausting. All of that is in his writing.

Given Fritz's extreme states, it is surprising that the real power of his writing is its startling clarity; the bullseyes of emotional truth he finds. "The shadows are the first to go," is the first line of *The World Next Door*—Fritz claimed e. e. cummings said it was "the best first sentence in the history of the English language."[24] Fritz's writing is true, and clear, and evocative; also, readable. Fritz desired "always to be known as a readable writer rather than a great artist."[25] There is something of Gurdjieff's teachings and character in the pragmatism, the immediacy, the uncompromising search for truth and self, that is at the heart of it.

But the biggest tragedy of mental instability, which Fritz captures in *The World Next Door*, is being unable to understand, or control, the way one hurts people. "Seeing ourselves how others see us," as Gurdjieff would put it—is a challenge for everyone, but especially for those with a tenuous grasp on "self." Even in his healthiest and happiest moments, Fritz spent his life in this exile. He wrote to us from the electroshock table, from the queer underground, from

---

24 Jane Madeline Gold, *Down from Above, Up from Below* (Rhinebeck: Epigraph Books, 2021), 25.

25 Richard H. Costa, "Author Pens Tale of Route 20," *Utica Observer-Dispatch*, December 10, 1950.

puberty, from the side of the road, from a marriage on its last leg, from the rubble of World War II, from Gurdjieff's intentional community. Fritz went there and reported back—that was his gift.

FRITZ PETERS
1913 – 1979

Born in Madison, Wisconsin, Arthur Anderson "Fritz" Peters was the author of both novels and memoirs, which touched on themes of spirituality, mental illness, homosexuality, self and society, always through the lens of an unrelenting individuality and nonconformism.

Peters' most successful novel was *Finistère*, published in 1951, which sold over 350,000 copies and was an influential and unapologetic work of early gay literature. Due to instability in his family life, Peters spent his childhood between Europe and the United States, often nurtured by those adults who were able and willing to assist.

Central to his upbringing was his aunt Margaret Anderson and her partner Jane Heap, creators of *The Little Review* literary magazine, along with other members of their circle, such as Gertrude Stein. Most notably, the esoteric teacher Georges Gurdjieff interacted closely with Fritz from an early age and was hugely influential in Peters' life and literature. *Boyhood with Gurdjieff*, Peters' most popular memoir, paints these figures and their projects in a thoughtful and intimate light.

ABOUT THE PUBLISHER

VANITAS VANITATUM
PUBLISHING
LOS ANGELES

Vanitas Vanitatum Publishing is the literary wing of Vanitas Vanitatum Entertainment – an L.A. based production company built on instinct, courage, and craft. It was founded in 2025 by Giovanni J. Guidotti, CEO of Giovanni Eco Chic Beauty.

The Fritz Peters Collection was originally republished in 2024 by Hirsch Giovanni Entertainment + Publishing, which was founded by Guidotti and Hollywood industry veteran David M. Hirsch.